"Franchising in Asia – Unlocking Growth in the World's Most Dynamic Region"

by
Sean Flynn

Table of Contents

About the Author

Sean Flynn is a franchise professional with over 30 years in the business. He qualified as a Certified Franchise Executive (CFE) in 2013 and earned his Lean Six Sigma Black Belt more recently. His first book, "Franchise Success: Unlocking the Path to Business Expansion" was published on Amazon in 2024.

He began his career in franchising in Canada working at The Keg restaurant group while attending University. A job to earn some extra money to pay for tuition became a life-long pursuit of franchising excellence.

Intrigued with the franchise model, he moved to Singapore and took on the role of head of marketing for the Master Franchisee for Pizza Hut in Singapore and Malaysia. It wasn't long before his ambition and enthusiasm saw him promoted to the Country Manager role for Pizza Hut Singapore at 27 years of age. The objective there was pure growth. They grew from 4 to over 40 outlets in under five years.

Following that success, he then joined a company that held the Master Franchise for A&W Restaurants in Singapore and Thailand. With only 27 units in total, the company was losing money and needed to be turned around. A focused effort on improving operations issues such as menu engineering, labour control, effective marketing, opening new high-impact locations and closing poor locations resulted in a multi-million-dollar turnaround in under 2 years. It was profitable again.

But the overriding lesson was learning precisely what the franchisees needs from the franchisor, and just as importantly, what they do not! Their respective interests were simply not aligned, in fact, they were often in conflict.

His experience leading on the franchisor side of the equation began with his Presidency of the 73-unit Shakey's Pizza business based in Los Angeles. Here he found the love for brand leadership. Implementing the lessons learned previously, he engaged with the franchise community and reimagined the brand through new menu innovations and prototype development. Shakey's even began growing the franchise network again for the first time in decades.

Moving back to Canada, he then became President of Smitty's Family Restaurants which had close to 100 units when he joined. Again, the focus on improving the performance and stability of this business centred around adding value to the franchise community through branding, systems, menu development, and supply chain initiatives. It wasn't long before both the franchisees and the franchisors were seeing vastly improved performance on top and bottom lines. The business started growing again and topped 120 units in 3 years.

Both Shakey's and Smitty's were mature brands, having been in business for about 40+ years. There were plenty of legacy issues and lessons to be learned about the pitfalls of older franchise models that failed to align the franchisee/ franchisor interests.

Sean then moved back to Singapore for personal reasons. There he had an incredible opportunity to create a fresh and modern franchise business with the Brotzeit – German Bier Bar and Restaurant concept. As the CEO of the business, he led the creation of a thoroughly modern franchise model that incorporated everything he had learned about the business over the previous 25 years. Brotzeit became the gold standard in the franchise business. In under 3 years, he and his team built a comprehensive infrastructure and franchising program which saw the establishment of franchise operations in Malaysia, Hong Kong, Vietnam, Thailand, Shanghai, Beijing, the Philippines, and Australia. Brotzeit remain the world's largest German franchise concept. Brotzeit won the "Franchise of the Year" award in 2012 from the Franchise & Licencing Association of Singapore.

Since that time, and now based in Vancouver Canada, Sean has been helping client companies in all aspects of franchise development and growth. He has helped to build franchise platforms for several F&B concepts, as well as Hotel and Serviced Residence concepts in Singapore, Bali, China, and Canada. This has allowed him to share his experience to help companies and brands truly understand winning strategies in franchising.

Visit his website at www.dsflynn.com.

"The best way to predict the future is to create it."

Abraham Lincoln

Introduction
The Asian Franchise Landscape

A Symphony of Opportunity and Challenge

Picture a bustling street in Bangkok, where the aroma of sizzling Pad Thai mingles with the scent of freshly brewed coffee from a well-known Western chain. Nearby, a local bubble tea franchise sees a queue of young professionals spilling onto the sidewalk. This scene, replicated with variations across thousands of cities in Asia, encapsulates the vibrant and complex world of franchising in this diverse continent.

The Asian franchise landscape is a tapestry woven from threads of tradition and modernity, local flavours and global brands, presenting a panorama of opportunity tinged with unique challenges. From the neon-lit streets of Tokyo to the chaotic bazaars of Mumbai, franchising has become an integral part of the Asian business ecosystem, evolving into a force that shapes economies and cultures alike.

A Journey Through Time

The story of franchising in Asia is one of rapid transformation. In the 1970s and 1980s, Western brands like McDonald's and KFC planted their flags in Asian soil, often greeted with a mixture of curiosity and scepticism. These golden arches and smiling colonels were harbingers of a new era, introducing not just new flavours but entire business models to the region.

As we moved into the 1990s and 2000s, a new chapter began. Local entrepreneurs, inspired by the success of these foreign imports, began crafting their own franchise concepts. Brands like Jollibee in the Philippines and Yoshinoya in Japan showed that Asian companies could play the franchise game just as well as their Western counterparts, often with a deeper understanding of local palates and preferences.

Today, the Asian franchise landscape is a melting pot where East meets West, tradition blends with innovation, and local champions stand shoulder to shoulder with global giants. It's a market estimated at a staggering US$1.3 trillion as of 2023, growing at a pace that outstrips many other regions of the world.

A Mosaic of Markets

To understand franchising in Asia is to appreciate its diversity. Each country presents a unique ecosystem, shaped by its culture, economy, and regulatory environment.

China, with its vast population and rapidly growing middle class, is a franchise powerhouse. Here, the sheer scale of opportunity is matched only by the complexity of navigating its business landscape. In bustling cities like Shanghai and Shenzhen, franchises must compete for attention in a sea of options, while also expanding into second and third-tier cities hungry for new experiences.

Japan and South Korea present a different picture. These mature markets boast sophisticated consumers with high expectations for quality and service. Here, franchises must constantly innovate to stay relevant, leading to concepts that often seem futuristic to Western eyes.

Southeast Asia is a region of contrasts. In Singapore, a compact city-state with an affluent population, franchises operate in a highly regulated but supportive environment. Just a short flight away, in the sprawling archipelago of Indonesia, franchisees grapple with logistical challenges while tapping into a market of over 270 million people.

India, often described as a continent within a country, presents its own unique tapestry. Here, franchises must navigate a complex web of regional preferences, adapting everything from their menus to their marketing strategies as they move from the tech hubs of Bangalore to the traditional markets of Jaipur.

The Flavour of Success

While the landscape is diverse, certain ingredients seem to be part of every successful franchise recipe in Asia. Adaptation is key - the ability to tweak concepts to local tastes without losing the core brand identity. Take, for example, how Pizza Hut offers durian pizza in Malaysia, or how Dunkin' Donuts serves dry pork and seaweed donuts in China.

Relationship-building is another crucial element. In many Asian cultures, business is personal. Successful franchisors invest time in understanding the local culture, building trust with franchisees, and often working with family-owned businesses that form the backbone of many Asian economies.

Technology, too, plays an increasingly vital role. From mobile ordering apps to AI-driven customer service, franchises that embrace digital innovation often find themselves at the forefront of their sectors. In countries like South Korea and China, a strong digital presence isn't just an advantage - it's a necessity.

Challenges on the Horizon

Yet, for all its promise, the Asian franchise landscape is not without its thorns. Intellectual property protection remains a concern in several markets, with some local businesses quick to imitate successful concepts. Navigating the regulatory environment can be a labyrinthine task, with rules varying not just between countries but sometimes between cities within the same country.

Cultural and linguistic barriers present another hurdle. A marketing campaign that resonates in Tokyo might fall flat in Jakarta. Even within countries, regional differences can be stark - what works in North India might not translate to the South.

Looking to the Future

As we peer into the future, the Asian franchise landscape continues to evolve. Sustainability is becoming a key focus, with consumers increasingly favouring brands that demonstrate environmental and social responsibility. The rise of multi-brand franchisees and investment groups is changing the power dynamics in the industry. And regional trade agreements are slowly but surely making cross-border franchising more feasible.

From the tech-savvy youth of Seoul to the aspiring middle class of Mumbai, from the food courts of Singapore to the shopping malls of Shanghai, the story of franchising in Asia is still being written. It's a narrative of ambition and adaptation, of global brands and local ingenuity, of challenges overcome and opportunities seized.

For those willing to navigate its complexities, the Asian franchise landscape offers a world of possibility - a chance to be part of one of the most dynamic business environments on the planet. In the chapters that follow, we'll dive deeper into each market, exploring the nuances that make franchising in Asia a journey like no other.

Why Franchise in Asia?

A Land of Promise and Potential

Imagine standing atop one of Singapore's iconic skyscrapers, gazing out at the city-state's gleaming skyline. Now, picture yourself in the heart of Hanoi's Old Quarter, surrounded by the buzz of motorbikes and the aroma of pho. Finally, envision the vast expanse of Mumbai's suburbs, teeming with millions of aspiring consumers. These diverse snapshots capture just a fraction of what makes Asia an irresistible frontier for franchising.

But why, you might ask, should one venture into this complex tapestry of cultures, economies, and regulations? The answer lies in a potent mixture of opportunity, growth, and transformation that is uniquely Asian.

The Economic Powerhouse

Asia's economic narrative is nothing short of extraordinary. For decades, the region has been the world's economic engine, consistently outpacing global growth rates. China's meteoric rise may have grabbed headlines, but it's far from the only story. From the technological prowess of South Korea to the manufacturing might of Vietnam, from the service excellence of Singapore to the IT hubs of India, Asia presents a diverse economic landscape ripe with opportunity.

This economic vigour translates directly into franchising potential. As disposable incomes rise, so does the appetite for new products, services, and experiences. The middle class in Asia is not just growing; it's evolving, developing sophisticated tastes and a hunger for both local and international brands. For franchisors, this represents an unparalleled opportunity to tap into markets that are not just large but also increasingly affluent and brand conscious.

A Demographic Dividend

Asia's population story is equally compelling. Home to nearly 60% of the world's people, the region offers scale that is hard to match. But it's not just about numbers. Asia boasts a youthful population, particularly in countries like India, Indonesia, and Vietnam. This demographic dividend presents franchisors with a customer base that is not only large but also dynamic, tech-savvy, and open to new concepts.

Moreover, rapid urbanization across the region is creating new centres of consumption. Second and third-tier cities in China and India, for instance, represent vast untapped markets. For franchises willing to venture beyond the obvious metropolitan hubs, the rewards can be substantial.

A Culture of Entrepreneurship

Asia has long been a hotbed of entrepreneurial spirit. From family-owned businesses that span generations to tech startups disrupting traditional industries, the region pulses with entrepreneurial energy. This culture aligns perfectly with the franchise model, which essentially empowers entrepreneurs to run their own businesses under the umbrella of an established brand.

In many Asian countries, becoming a franchisee is seen as a respected path to business ownership, offering a blend of independence and support that is particularly appealing in cultures that value both individual achievement and community ties.

Technological Leapfrogging

One of Asia's most exciting attributes is its ability to leapfrog outdated technologies and embrace cutting-edge solutions. Many Asian consumers, for instance, skipped the personal computer era and went straight to smartphones. This technological agility creates fertile ground for franchises, especially those with strong digital components.

From mobile payment systems that make cash obsolete in Chinese cities to AI-driven customer service chatbots in South Korea, Asia often serves as a testing ground for innovations that later spread globally. For franchises, this means an opportunity to not just expand geographically, but to evolve and future-proof their business models.

A Gateway to Global Growth

Success in Asia can be a springboard to global recognition. The sheer size and diversity of Asian markets mean that a franchise that thrives here has essentially stress-tested its model under a wide range of conditions. A restaurant chain that can satisfy palates from Tokyo to Jakarta, or a service franchise that can operate efficiently in both the hyper-organized environment of Singapore and the more fluid business landscape of India, proves its adaptability and resilience.

Moreover, as Asian brands increasingly look to expand globally, partnering with local franchisees can provide valuable insights and connections for future international growth.

Challenges as Opportunities

It would be remiss not to mention the challenges of franchising in Asia – the regulatory complexities, the cultural nuances, the intense competition. Yet, it's precisely these challenges that make success in Asia so rewarding. They necessitate innovation, foster adaptability, and ultimately create stronger, more resilient franchise systems.

For instance, the need to adapt menus or service offerings to local tastes often leads to innovations that can be exported back to a franchise's home market. The stringent quality expectations of Japanese consumers or the value-consciousness of Indian customers can drive improvements in product design and operational efficiency that benefit the entire franchise system globally.

A Canvas for Innovation

Finally, Asia presents a unique canvas for innovative franchise concepts. The region's blend of ancient traditions and cutting-edge modernity, its dense urban centres and vast rural expanses, its young digital natives and revered elders – all these contrasts create niches for novel franchise ideas.

Whether it's a franchise that combines traditional herbal medicine with modern wellness trends, or one that brings high-tech vending machine concepts to rural areas, Asia provides both the inspiration and the market for innovative thinking in franchising.

In essence, franchising in Asia is not just about expanding a business; it's about being part of one of the most dynamic and transformative chapters in global economic history. It's a journey that challenges, inspires, and rewards in equal measure, offering those who embark upon it a chance to not just grow their business, but to reimagine what their business could be.

As we delve deeper into the specifics of each market in the coming chapters, keep in mind this overarching truth: in the vast and varied landscape of Asian franchising, every challenge conceals an opportunity, and every cultural difference holds the potential for innovation. For those with the vision to see it and the adaptability to seize it, Asia is not just a market – it's a world of possibilities waiting to be explored.

Overview of Key Markets

A Kaleidoscope of Opportunities

From the neon-lit streets of Tokyo to the sun-drenched beaches of Bali, from the high-tech corridors of Seoul to the ancient alleyways of Delhi, each market presents a unique tapestry of challenges and opportunities.

Let's embark on a whirlwind tour of these diverse landscapes, each a world unto itself, yet part of the greater Asian franchising mosaic.

The Dragon Awakened: China

China, with its population of 1.4 billion, is the behemoth of Asian markets. Here, scale takes on new meaning. A "small" city might have more inhabitants than some entire countries. The pace of change is dizzying – skylines transform overnight, and consumer trends shift at lightning speed.

In this land of contrasts, ancient traditions coexist with cutting-edge technology. WeChat Pay and Alipay have made cash almost obsolete in major cities, while high-speed trains whisk people between megacities at mind-boggling velocities. For franchises, China offers unparalleled scale but demands equal measures of adaptability and cultural sensitivity.

Success stories like Starbucks, which turned a nation of tea drinkers into coffee aficionados, demonstrate the potential. But the landscape is littered with casualties too – brands that underestimated the importance of localization or the complexity of Chinese regulations. In China, the franchise journey is not for the faint-hearted, but for those who navigate it successfully, the rewards can be astronomical.

The Land of the Rising Sun: Japan

Japan presents a study in contrasts to China. Here, in a market known for its sophistication and attention to detail, quality reigns supreme. The Japanese consumer is discerning, loyal, and willing to pay a premium for excellence.

This is a mature market where robots serve in restaurants, and vending machines offer everything from hot meals to umbrellas. For franchises, Japan is both a challenge and an inspiration. The level of service expected here often sets global standards. A franchise that can satisfy Japanese consumers often finds itself well-prepared for any market in the world.

But Japan is not just about high-tech and efficiency. It's also a culture that deeply values tradition and craftsmanship. Successful franchises here often find ways to blend the new with the old, respecting local customs while introducing innovative concepts.

The Tiger Economy: South Korea

South Korea, often overshadowed by its larger neighbours, is a franchise powerhouse in its own right. This is a country where trends can sweep the nation overnight, driven by a hyper-connected, tech-savvy population.

The franchise landscape in Korea is incredibly dynamic. Local brands like Paris Baguette have not only dominated the domestic market but have successfully expanded overseas. International franchises entering Korea often find themselves competing not just on product quality, but on technological integration and speed of service.

Korea's unique "ppalli-ppalli" (hurry-hurry) culture demands efficiency, while its communal dining traditions influence restaurant layouts and menu designs. For franchises, Korea offers a market that's always hungry for the next big thing, but also one that expects flawless execution.

The Melting Pot: Singapore

Singapore, the tiny city-state with an oversized impact, serves as a microcosm of Asian franchising. Its diverse population, comprising Chinese, Malay, Indian, and Western expatriate communities, makes it an ideal testing ground for concepts destined for wider Asian expansion.

Here, in one of the world's most business-friendly environments, franchises benefit from strong intellectual property protection and a government that actively supports the industry. The challenge in Singapore isn't navigating red tape – it's standing out in a market saturated with options.

From the hawker centres serving traditional street food to the glitzy malls housing international luxury brands, Singapore embodies the coexistence of old and new that characterizes much of Asia. Franchises that succeed here often master the art of appealing to both tradition-loving locals and cosmopolitan expatriates.

The Sleeping Giant: India

India, with its 1.3 billion people, presents a franchise landscape as diverse as its population. This is not one market, but many — each state akin to a different country, with its own language, culture, and consumer preferences.

The potential in India is enormous, but so are the challenges. Infrastructure issues, complex regulations that vary by state, and a vast population with wildly different income levels all add to the complexity. Yet, for franchises that crack the code, the rewards are immense.

Success in India often comes to those who master the art of localization. McDonald's serves vegetarian-only restaurants in some regions, while Domino's has found success with pizzas topped with tandoori chicken. In India, adaptability isn't just an advantage — it's a necessity.

The Rising Star: Vietnam

Vietnam represents the new wave of Asian economic development. With a young population, rapidly growing middle class, and increasing urbanization, it's a market brimming with potential for franchises.

Here, the franchise industry is still in its early stages, offering first-mover advantages in many sectors. The country's love affair with motorbikes has even spawned drive-through models designed specifically for two-wheelers.

But Vietnam is not just about opportunity — it's also about complexity. Navigating relationships with local partners, understanding the nuances of a post-communist economy, and adapting to a market where street food still reigns supreme all present unique challenges.

A Continent of Contrasts

Each of these markets – and the others we'll explore in depth later – offers its own unique flavour of opportunity and challenge. From the well-established franchise markets of Australia and New Zealand to the emerging landscapes of Indonesia and the Philippines, from the economic powerhouse of Thailand to the rapidly evolving marketplace of Malaysia, Asia presents a continent of contrasts.

What unites these diverse markets is the pace of change, the scale of opportunity, and the need for nuanced understanding. A franchise that succeeds in the hyper-competitive landscape of Hong Kong may need a completely different approach in the more relationship-driven business environment of Jakarta.

As we delve deeper into each of these markets in the coming chapters, we'll uncover the specific strategies, cultural insights, and operational tactics needed to navigate them successfully. We'll explore how global brands have adapted to local tastes, and how homegrown Asian franchises have expanded beyond their borders.

Remember, in the world of Asian franchising, there's no one-size-fits-all approach. Each market is a world unto itself, requiring a blend of global best practices and local insights. But for those willing to embrace this complexity, to learn and adapt, the Asian franchise landscape offers a universe of opportunity unlike any other in the world.

Understanding Franchising in Asia

Cultural Considerations

The Invisible Hand of Culture

In Asia, culture isn't just about traditions and customs; it's the invisible hand that shapes consumer behaviour, business practices, and social interactions. For franchises venturing into this diverse region, understanding and respecting these cultural nuances isn't just good manners – it's a critical success factor.

The Mosaic of Asian Values

Asia is far from a monolithic entity. Each country, indeed, each region within countries, has its own unique cultural fingerprint. However, certain broader cultural themes resonate across much of the continent, forming a complex mosaic of values that franchises must navigate.

Collectivism vs. Individualism

In many Asian societies, the needs of the group often trump individual desires. This collectivist mindset manifests in various ways that impact franchising. For instance, in Japan, group consensus is crucial in decision-making processes. A franchise looking to close a deal might find that while their primary contact seems enthusiastic, the final decision hinges on the approval of a larger team.

This collectivist approach also influences consumer behaviour. In South Korea, for example, the popularity of "chimaek" (chicken and beer) is as much about the social experience as it is about the food itself. Franchises that create spaces and experiences catering to group dynamics often find greater success.

Face and Social Harmony

The concept of "face" – maintaining dignity and social standing – is paramount in many Asian cultures. In China, giving or losing face can make or break business relationships. A franchise that publicly criticizes a local partner, even if justified, might find doors closing across the entire market.

This emphasis on social harmony also means that conflict resolution often takes place behind the scenes. In countries like Thailand or Vietnam, a smiling face doesn't always indicate agreement. Franchisors need to develop a keen sense for reading between the lines and addressing issues indirectly to maintain harmonious relationships.

Hierarchy and Respect for Authority

Many Asian societies have a more pronounced hierarchical structure than their Western counterparts. Age, position, and social status carry significant weight. In a franchise context, this might mean that the most senior person in the room expects to be addressed first, even if they're not the primary decision-maker.

This respect for hierarchy extends to brand perception as well. In markets like Japan or South Korea, established brands often command a level of respect and loyalty that can be challenging for newcomers to overcome. Conversely, in emerging markets like Vietnam or Indonesia, Western brands might be automatically perceived as premium, regardless of their positioning in their home countries.

The Role of Relationships

Across much of Asia, business is personal. The Western notion of separating professional and personal lives often doesn't apply. In China, the concept of "guanxi" – the network of relationships and mutual obligations – can be crucial to business success. A franchise might find that investing time in building personal relationships with partners, suppliers, and even government officials pay dividends in the long run.

This relationship-centric approach also extends to customer service. In markets like Singapore or Hong Kong, customers often expect a level of personalized service that goes beyond the transactional. Successful franchises in these markets often invest heavily in training staff to build lasting relationships with customers.

Time and Patience

The perception and value of time vary significantly across Asian cultures. In Japan, punctuality is paramount, and being late is considered deeply disrespectful. In contrast, in India or Indonesia, a more fluid approach to time is common. For franchises, this might mean adapting operational processes to local time cultures – whether that's ensuring split-second efficiency in Tokyo or building in buffer time for meetings in Jakarta.

Moreover, many Asian cultures take a long-term view of business relationships. Quick wins might be less valued than the promise of long-term stability and growth. Franchises often find that patience – in negotiations, in market development, in relationship-building – is not just a virtue but a necessity.

Language and Communication

While English is widely used in business across much of Asia, the importance of local languages cannot be overstated. In markets like China or Japan, having materials and contracts in the local language isn't just a courtesy – it's often a legal requirement.

But language considerations go beyond mere translation. The way information is communicated can be just as important as the content itself. In many Asian cultures, communication is high context, relying heavily on non-verbal cues and what is left unsaid. A franchise used to the direct communication styles of the West might find itself missing crucial information if it fails to read between the lines.

Culinary Cultures and Food Taboos

For food and beverage franchises, understanding local culinary cultures is paramount. What works in one market might be unpalatable in another. Pork, a staple in many Western cuisines, is taboo in Muslim-majority countries like Malaysia or Indonesia. Beef, while popular in many countries, is problematic in India where cows are considered sacred by many.

But it's not just about avoiding taboos. Successfully adapting to local tastes can lead to remarkable success stories. Pizza Hut's durian pizza in Southeast Asia or McDonald's Teriyaki Burger in Japan are testament to the power of cultural adaptation in menu design.

Work Cultures and Management Styles

The way people work and expect to be managed varies significantly across Asia. In Japan, the concept of "nemawashi" – building consensus before a formal decision – is crucial. In contrast, in countries like India, a more hierarchical decision-making process might be the norm.

Employee expectations also differ. While work-life balance is becoming more important across the region, the definition of what that means varies. In South Korea, for instance, after-work socializing with colleagues is often considered part of the job, while in Singapore, employees might expect more defined boundaries between work and personal time.

Festivals and Holidays

Asia's rich tapestry of festivals and holidays presents both challenges and opportunities for franchises. Understanding the significance of events like Chinese New Year, Diwali, or Ramadan is crucial for everything from inventory management to marketing campaigns.

These cultural events often come with specific consumer behaviours. For instance, the gift-giving culture during Chinese New Year can be a boon for retail franchises, while the fasting month of Ramadan significantly alters eating patterns in Muslim-majority countries.

The Digital Culture Divide

While much of Asia is at the forefront of digital adoption, the way technology is used and perceived varies greatly. In China, for example, super-apps like WeChat are central to daily life, handling everything from social messaging to payments. In contrast, in Japan, while technologically advanced in many ways, there's still a surprising reliance on cash and traditional paperwork in some sectors.

For franchises, understanding these digital cultural nuances is crucial. A digital strategy that works in hyper-connected South Korea might need significant adaptation in the more diverse digital landscape of India.

Navigating the Cultural Maze

As we've seen, the cultural considerations in Asian franchising are as diverse as the continent itself. What works in Tokyo might fall flat in Bangkok. A marketing campaign that resonates in Mumbai could be tone-deaf in Manila.

For franchises looking to succeed in Asia, cultural intelligence is not just an asset – it's a necessity. This means going beyond surface-level understanding to truly immerse oneself in the local context. It means being flexible enough to adapt not just products and services, but entire business models to align with local cultural norms.

But it's important to remember that culture is not static. Asia, perhaps more than any other region, is in a constant state of flux. Traditions blend with modernity, creating new cultural hybrids. Young consumers in Seoul or Shanghai might have more in common with their counterparts in Sydney or San Francisco than with their grandparents.

As we delve deeper into specific markets and sectors in the coming chapters, we'll explore how successful franchises navigate this complex cultural landscape. We'll see how global brands localize their offerings without losing their core identity, and how Asian franchises leverage cultural insights to expand both within the region and beyond.

In the end, the franchises that thrive in Asia are those that see cultural diversity not as a challenge to be overcome, but as a rich source of inspiration and opportunity. They are the ones who understand that in Asia, business is never just business – it's a cultural exchange, a meeting of worlds, and an ongoing journey of mutual understanding and adaptation.

Legal Frameworks

The Labyrinth of Laws

In this vast and varied continent, legal systems range from the common law traditions of Hong Kong and Singapore to the civil law systems of Japan and South Korea, from the socialist-influenced frameworks of China and Vietnam to the unique blend of common law and Sharia law in Malaysia. For franchises looking to expand across Asia, navigating this legal labyrinth is not just a compliance issue – it's a strategic imperative.

The Patchwork of Regulations

Unlike the relatively harmonized franchise laws of the European Union or the overarching federal regulations in the United States, Asia presents a patchwork of legal frameworks, each with its own quirks and complexities.

China: The Dragon's Rules

In the world's most populous country, franchising is governed by a set of regulations that have evolved rapidly over the past two decades. The cornerstone is the Regulations on the Administration of Commercial Franchises, implemented in 2007 and further refined in subsequent years.

Key requirements include:

- ⇒ The "2+1" rule: Franchisors must have operated at least two company-owned outlets for more than a year before they can franchise in China.
- ⇒ Mandatory disclosure: Detailed information about the franchise system must be provided to potential franchisees at least 30 days before signing an agreement.

⇒ Registration: Franchisors must register with the Ministry of Commerce within 15 days of signing their first franchise agreement in China.

The interpretation and enforcement of these regulations can vary by region, adding another layer of complexity. A franchise that's compliant in Shanghai might find itself facing unexpected hurdles in Chengdu.

Japan: Precision and Disclosure

In the land of the rising sun, there is no specific franchise law. Instead, franchising falls under the broader umbrella of contract and commercial law. However, the Japan Fair Trade Commission has issued guidelines that have the practical effect of law.

These guidelines place a strong emphasis on disclosure. Franchisors are required to provide detailed and accurate information about their business, including:

⇒ Historical financial performance
⇒ Projected earnings (if provided, these must be based on reasonable assumptions)
⇒ Details of any territorial rights
⇒ Obligations of the franchisee, including fees and investments

Failure to provide accurate information can lead to the franchise agreement being nullified, even years after it was signed. In a culture that values precision and honesty, the consequences of misleading disclosure can be severe and long-lasting.

South Korea: The Franchise-Friendly Tiger

South Korea has one of the most developed legal frameworks for franchising in Asia. The Fair Transactions in Franchise Business Act, first enacted in 2002 and subsequently amended, provides comprehensive regulation of franchise activities.

Key features include:

⇒ Mandatory disclosure: Franchisors must provide a disclosure document at least 14 days before signing an agreement or receiving any payment.
⇒ Cooling-off period: Franchisees have a 14-day period after signing the agreement during which they can cancel without penalty.
⇒ Registration: Franchisors must register their disclosure document with the Korea Fair Trade Commission.

South Korea's framework is generally seen as franchise-friendly, providing clear guidelines while also offering protection for franchisees. This clarity has contributed to the robust growth of both domestic and international franchise brands in the country.

India: The Federal-State Dance

In the world's largest democracy, franchising operates in a legal environment that's as diverse as the country itself. There's no specific federal franchise law, but various aspects of franchising are governed by a multitude of existing laws, including:

⇒ The Contract Act
⇒ The Trademarks Act
⇒ The Copyright Act
⇒ The Competition Act

Moreover, individual states have the power to enact laws that affect franchising, leading to a situation where compliance in one state doesn't guarantee compliance nationwide. For instance, labour laws or shop and establishment acts can vary significantly from state to state.

Foreign franchisors must also navigate India's foreign direct investment (FDI) regulations, which can restrict foreign ownership in certain sectors. This often leads to creative structuring of franchise agreements to comply with both franchise best practices and FDI rules.

Southeast Asia: A Mosaic of Approaches

The countries of Southeast Asia present a diverse range of legal approaches to franchising:

⇒ Malaysia has a specific franchise law, the Franchise Act 1998, which requires franchisors to register with the Franchise Registry before selling franchises.

⇒ Indonesia introduced specific franchise regulations in 2007, requiring registration and imposing local content requirements.

⇒ Vietnam has regulations on commercial franchising under its Commercial Law, requiring registration of franchise agreements with the Ministry of Industry and Trade.

⇒ Thailand, the Philippines, and Singapore don't have specific franchise laws but regulate franchising through various existing commercial and investment laws.

This diversity means that a one-size-fits-all approach to Southeast Asian expansion is rarely feasible. A franchise agreement that works in Singapore might need significant modification for use in Malaysia or Indonesia.

The Intellectual Property Conundrum

Across Asia, the protection of intellectual property (IP) – a cornerstone of franchising – varies widely in both law and practice. While countries like Singapore and Japan have strong IP protection regimes, enforcement can be challenging in other markets.

China, often cited as a challenging market for IP protection, has made significant strides in recent years, but enforcement can still be inconsistent. In emerging markets like Vietnam or Indonesia, the legal framework for IP protection exists, but practical enforcement can be an uphill battle.

For franchisors, this means that IP protection strategies need to be tailored to each market. This might involve:

⇒ Aggressive trademark registration, even for marks not immediately planned for use
⇒ Careful structuring of franchise agreements to maximize IP protection
⇒ Ongoing monitoring and swift action against infringements
⇒ The Evolving Landscape

If there's one constant in the legal frameworks for franchising in Asia, it's change. As economies develop and governments recognize the economic potential of franchising, laws and regulations are continually evolving.

For instance:

⇒ China regularly updates its franchise regulations, often in response to issues that arise in the market.
⇒ India has been considering a specific franchise law for years, which could significantly alter the landscape if enacted.
⇒ Countries like Vietnam and Indonesia frequently refine their foreign investment regulations, which can have knock-on effects for international franchisors.
⇒ This dynamic environment means that franchisors must remain vigilant, regularly reviewing and updating their legal strategies. What was compliant yesterday might not be tomorrow.

Navigating the Legal Maze

Given this complex and dynamic legal landscape, how can franchisors successfully navigate expansion in Asia? Several strategies emerge:

⇒ Local Expertise is Non-Negotiable
Partnering with local legal experts who understand both the letter of the law and its practical application is crucial. These

partners can provide invaluable insights into local nuances and help anticipate potential issues.

⇒ Flexibility in Franchise Structures
The traditional master franchise model may not always be the best fit given local regulations. Franchisors need to be open to alternative structures, such as area development agreements or joint ventures, to comply with local laws while achieving their expansion goals.

⇒ Thorough Due Diligence
Before entering any Asian market, comprehensive legal due diligence is essential. This goes beyond just understanding franchise-specific laws to encompass the broader legal and regulatory environment that will impact operations.

⇒ Customized Agreements
While it's tempting to use a standardized franchise agreement across markets, the diverse legal frameworks in Asia often necessitate significant customization. A one-size-fits-all approach is rarely effective.

⇒ Ongoing Compliance Monitoring
Given the evolving nature of laws and regulations, franchisors need systems in place to monitor legal changes and assess their impact on operations. This might involve regular legal audits and close collaboration with local legal partners.

⇒ Dispute Resolution Planning
Given the complexities of enforcing contracts across different legal systems, careful thought needs to be given to dispute resolution mechanisms. This might involve specifying neutral arbitration venues or tailoring dispute resolution clauses to local realities.

The Road Ahead

As we venture deeper into specific markets and sectors in the coming chapters, we'll explore how successful franchises have navigated these complex legal waters. We'll see case studies of brands that have adeptly adapted their models to comply with local laws while maintaining their core identity and standards.

Remember, in the world of Asian franchising, legal compliance isn't just about avoiding pitfalls – it's about creating a solid foundation for sustainable growth. The franchisors who thrive are those who see legal frameworks not as obstacles, but as guideposts helping them chart a course through the rich and rewarding landscape of Asian markets.

In this ever-changing legal terrain, knowledge, adaptability, and respect for local laws aren't just virtues – they're the keys to unlocking the vast potential of franchising in Asia. As we move forward, keep in mind that every legal challenge overcome is a step closer to success in one of the world's most dynamic and promising franchise markets.

Economic Factors

The Economic Tapestry of Asia

For franchises looking to expand in Asia, understanding this economic tapestry is crucial. The region isn't just a collection of markets; it's a complex ecosystem of interconnected economies, each at its own stage of development, each with its unique challenges and opportunities.

The Growth Engine

Asia has been the world's economic growth engine for decades, and this trend shows no signs of slowing. According to the Asian Development Bank, developing Asia is expected to grow by 6.2% in 2024, far outpacing global averages. But this growth isn't evenly distributed.

The Giants: China and India

China, the world's second-largest economy, continues to be a powerhouse despite a slowdown from its earlier breakneck pace. Its transition from an export-led model to one driven by domestic consumption presents both challenges and opportunities for franchises. The rise of a vast middle class with increasing disposable income has created a hungry market for everything from fast food to luxury goods.

India, often seen as the next economic superpower, presents a different picture. With its younger population and rapidly digitalizing economy, India offers a massive market potential. However, its economic development is more uneven, with stark contrasts between urban and rural areas, presenting unique challenges for franchises in terms of market penetration and adaptation.

The Tigers and Cubs

The "Asian Tigers" – Singapore, Hong Kong, South Korea, and Taiwan – have long been models of export-driven economic development. Now, they're transitioning to knowledge-based economies, driving innovation in sectors from fintech to biotech. For franchises, these markets offer sophisticated consumers and robust infrastructure, but also intense competition and high operational costs.

The "Tiger Cubs" – countries like Indonesia, Vietnam, and the Philippines – are following in the Tigers' footsteps. With young populations, increasing urbanization, and growing middle classes, these markets present significant growth opportunities for franchises willing to navigate their still-developing economic structures.

Japan: The Mature Market

Japan, the world's third-largest economy, presents a unique case. With an aging population and mature market, it offers stability and sophisticated consumers but also challenges in terms of growth. For franchises, success in Japan often requires a high degree of localization and attention to quality.

The Middle-Income Trap and Beyond

Several Asian economies, such as Malaysia and Thailand, are grappling with the "middle-income trap" – the challenge of transitioning from resource-driven growth to innovation-driven development. This transition creates both opportunities and challenges for franchises, as consumer behaviours and market dynamics evolve.

Economic Diversity and Disparity

One of the defining features of Asia's economic landscape is its diversity. The region encompasses some of the world's richest countries (like Singapore) and some of its poorest (like Myanmar). This diversity means that franchises must be prepared to operate across a wide spectrum of economic conditions, often within the same country.

In China, for instance, the economic realities of tier-one cities like Shanghai or Beijing are vastly different from those of tier-three or four cities. A franchise strategy that works in cosmopolitan Singapore might need significant adjustment for the more diverse Indonesian market.

This economic disparity also manifests in income inequality within countries. In many Asian markets, a small, affluent urban population coexists with a much larger, lower-income rural population. For franchises, this often necessitates a multi-tiered approach, with different offerings and pricing strategies for different market segments.

Consumption Patterns and the Rise of the Asian Middle Class

Perhaps the most significant economic factor driving franchising growth in Asia is the meteoric rise of the middle class. According to the Brookings Institution, by 2030, Asia will represent 66% of the global middle-class population and 59% of middle-class consumption.

This burgeoning middle class is characterized by:

⇒ Increasing disposable income
⇒ Growing appetite for international brands
⇒ Rising health and quality consciousness
⇒ Rapid adoption of digital technologies

For franchises, this presents a golden opportunity. Sectors like food and beverage, education, healthcare, and lifestyle services are seeing explosive growth. However, capturing this opportunity requires understanding the nuances of Asian middle-class consumption:

⇒ Value consciousness: Despite rising incomes, many Asian consumers remain highly value-conscious, expecting quality at competitive prices.

⇒ Brand loyalty: In many Asian markets, consumers show strong brand loyalty, but are also quick to embrace new concepts that resonate with their aspirations.

⇒ Localization preferences: While there's an appetite for international brands, success often hinges on effectively localizing offerings to suit local tastes and customs.

Digital Economy and E-commerce Boom

Asia is at the forefront of the global digital revolution. Countries like China, South Korea, and Singapore are world leaders in digital infrastructure and e-commerce adoption. Even in emerging markets like Indonesia and Vietnam, mobile internet penetration is driving rapid e-commerce growth.

For franchises, this digital boom presents both opportunities and challenges:

⇒ Omnichannel presence becomes crucial, with seamless integration between physical stores and digital platforms.

⇒ Social media and influencer marketing take on outsized importance in many Asian markets.

⇒ Digital payment systems, from China's WeChat Pay to India's UPI, are becoming the norm, requiring franchises to adapt their payment infrastructures.

Economic Policies and Foreign Investment

Government economic policies play a significant role in shaping the franchise landscape across Asia. Many countries have adopted policies to attract foreign investment, but these often come with conditions:

⇒ Local partnership requirements in sectors like retail and food service in countries like Indonesia and Malaysia.
⇒ Restrictions on foreign ownership in certain sectors, necessitating creative partnership structures.
⇒ Incentives for investment in particular regions or industries, influencing location strategies for franchises.

Understanding these policies and their implications is crucial for franchises planning expansion in Asia.

Currency Fluctuations and Economic Volatility

While many Asian economies have shown remarkable resilience, the region is not immune to global economic headwinds. Currency fluctuations can significantly impact franchise operations, affecting everything from royalty payments to supply chain costs.

Moreover, economic shocks – whether global events like the COVID-19 pandemic or regional issues like political changes – can have profound effects on consumer behaviour and market dynamics. Successful franchises in Asia need to build flexibility and resilience into their business models to navigate these uncertainties.

Labor Markets and Human Capital

Asia's labour markets are as diverse as its economies. Franchises must navigate a spectrum of challenges:

⇒ In developed markets like Japan and Singapore, labour shortages and high costs are significant issues.
⇒ In emerging markets, finding and retaining skilled labour can be challenging, often requiring significant investment in training and development.
⇒ Cultural factors, such as hierarchical structures in many Asian societies, can impact management styles and operational efficiency.

Understanding these labour market dynamics is crucial for franchises, particularly in service-oriented sectors where human capital is a key differentiator.

The Belt and Road Initiative and Regional Integration

China's Belt and Road Initiative (BRI) is reshaping economic landscapes across Asia. By investing in infrastructure and connectivity, the BRI is opening up new markets and creating new economic corridors. For franchises, this can mean easier access to previously challenging markets, but also increased competition as these markets become more connected to global trade networks.

Similarly, regional integration efforts like ASEAN (Association of Southeast Asian Nations) are creating larger, more unified markets. This integration presents opportunities for economies of scale but also requires franchises to think regionally rather than country-by-country in their expansion strategies.

Navigating the Economic Currents

Given this complex economic landscape, how can franchises successfully navigate expansion in Asia? Several strategies emerge:

⇒ Market Segmentation and Tiered Strategies
Recognizing the economic diversity within and between Asian markets, successful franchises often develop tiered strategies to cater to different market segments.

⇒ Localization with Global Standards
Balancing local adaptation with global brand consistency is key. This might involve developing market-specific products or services while maintaining core brand values and quality standards.

⇒ Digital Integration
Embracing digital technologies – from e-commerce platforms to digital payment systems – is crucial for success in Asia's tech-savvy markets.

⇒ Flexible Business Models
Given the diverse economic conditions, franchises need to be flexible in their business models, potentially adapting everything from store formats to franchise terms for different markets.

⇒ Long-term Vision with Short-term Adaptability
While it's important to have a long-term vision for Asian expansion, franchises also need the ability to adapt quickly to economic shifts and market changes.

⇒ Strategic Partnerships
Collaborating with local partners who understand the economic nuances of each market can be invaluable, providing insights and helping navigate local economic landscapes.

The Road Ahead

As we delve deeper into specific markets and sectors in the coming chapters, we'll explore how successful franchises have navigated these complex economic waters. We'll see case studies of brands that have adeptly adapted their models to thrive in Asia's diverse economic conditions.

Remember, in the world of Asian franchising, understanding economic factors isn't just about market analysis – it's about seeing the opportunities hidden in challenges, the potential in diversity, and the future in the present. The franchises that thrive are those who can read the economic currents, adapt to the flows, and chart a course through the rich and rewarding waters of Asian markets.

In this dynamic economic landscape, flexibility, insight, and a willingness to innovate aren't just advantageous – they're essential for unlocking the vast potential of franchising in Asia. As we move forward, keep in mind that every economic challenge overcome is a step closer to success in one of the world's most exciting and promising franchise markets.

China

Market Overview

The Middle Kingdom's Metamorphosis

China, with its population of 1.4 billion and an economy that has grown at an average of 9% per year since 1978, presents a tantalizing opportunity for franchises. The numbers are staggering:

⇒ GDP: $17.7 trillion (2021)
⇒ Middle class: Expected to reach 550 million by 2025
⇒ Urban population: 64% of total population (2021)
⇒ E-commerce market: Largest in the world, valued at $2.1 trillion in 2021

The franchise sector in China has experienced explosive growth. According to the China Chain Store & Franchise Association (CCFA), there were over 4,500 franchise systems operating in China as of 2021, with more than 400,000 franchised outlets.

Key sectors for franchising include:

⇒ Food and Beverage: From fast food to bubble tea, this sector continues to dominate.
⇒ Education: English language schools, after-school tutoring, and early childhood education are booming.
⇒ Retail: Both luxury brands and affordable fashion chains are expanding rapidly.
⇒ Services: Everything from fitness centres to beauty salons is seeing franchise growth.

The Chinese consumer is evolving rapidly. While price sensitivity remains a factor, there's growing emphasis on quality, brand reputation, and unique experiences. The post-90s generation, in particular, is driving trends towards premiumization and personalization.

Regulatory Environment

Navigating the Red Tape

The regulatory environment for franchising in China has come a long way since the first KFC opened its doors in Beijing in 1987. Today, franchising is governed by a complex web of laws and regulations, with the cornerstone being the Regulations on the Administration of Commercial Franchises (2007).

Key regulatory aspects include:

⇒ The "2+1" Rule: Franchisors must have operated at least two company-owned units for more than a year before they can franchise in China. This rule aims to prevent the franchising of untested business models.

⇒ Disclosure Requirements: Franchisors must provide prospective franchisees with a disclosure document at least 30 days before signing a franchise agreement. This document must include detailed information about the franchisor's business history, financial status, and existing franchisees.

⇒ Registration: Franchisors must register with the Ministry of Commerce (MOFCOM) within 15 days of signing their first franchise agreement in China.

⇒ Cooling-off Period: Franchisees have a right to unilaterally terminate the franchise agreement within a certain period (typically 30 days) after signing.

⇒ Trademark Registration: Franchisors must have a registered trademark in China before franchising. Given China's "first-to-file" system, securing trademark rights early is crucial.

⇒ Foreign Investment Restrictions: While many sectors are open to foreign franchisors, some (like compulsory education) remain restricted or prohibited.

The regulatory landscape is not static. Recent years have seen increased emphasis on data protection (with the implementation of the Personal Information Protection Law in 2021) and anti-monopoly regulations, which can affect large franchise networks.

Opportunities

The opportunities for franchising in China are as vast as the country itself:

⇒ Sheer Market Size: With a population larger than North America, the EU, and Russia combined, China offers unparalleled scale.

⇒ Rising Disposable Incomes: The average disposable income in urban areas has more than doubled in the past decade, fuelling consumer spending.

⇒ Urbanization: Ongoing urbanization is creating new markets in tier 2 and 3 cities, where competition is often less intense than in tier 1 megacities.

⇒ Digital Integration: China's advanced digital ecosystem, from mobile payments to social commerce, offers franchises powerful tools for customer engagement and operational efficiency.

⇒ Changing Consumer Preferences: Growing health consciousness, desire for international experiences, and emphasis on quality present opportunities for niche and premium concepts.

⇒ Government Support: Many local governments offer incentives for franchises that contribute to employment and economic development.

⇒ Belt and Road Initiative: This massive infrastructure project is opening up new markets and supply chain opportunities across Asia.

Challenges

Scaling the Great Wall

Despite the immense opportunities, franchising in China comes with significant challenges:

⇒ Cultural Adaptation: What works in the West often needs substantial modification for Chinese tastes and customs.

⇒ Intellectual Property Protection: While improving, IP infringement remains a concern. Vigilant monitoring and swift action are essential.

⇒ Finding Qualified Franchisees: With franchising still, a relatively new concept in many parts of China, finding partners with the right skills and capital can be challenging.

⇒ Regional Diversity: China is not a monolithic market. Consumer preferences, regulations, and business practices can vary significantly between regions.

⇒ Fierce Competition: Both from domestic brands and other international players. The Chinese market moves at lightning speed, with trends rising and falling rapidly.

⇒ Regulatory Compliance: Navigating the complex and sometimes opaque regulatory environment requires constant attention and local expertise.

⇒ Supply Chain Management: Ensuring consistent quality across a vast country with varying levels of infrastructure development can be daunting.

⇒ Labor Costs and Turnover: Rising wages in urban areas and high employee turnover rates pose challenges for labour-intensive franchise concepts.

Case Studies

Tales from the Franchise Frontier

Let's examine two contrasting case studies to illustrate the realities of franchising in China:

Case Study 1: KFC - The Localization Master

When KFC entered China in 1987, many doubted that a foreign fast-food chain could succeed in a country with a rich culinary tradition. Today, KFC has over 8,000 outlets in China, more than twice its presence in its home market of the United States.

Key to KFC's success:

⇒ Menu Localization: While maintaining its core fried chicken offering, KFC developed items like the "Dragon Twister" and congee to appeal to local tastes.
⇒ Rapid Expansion: KFC aggressively expanded into tier 2 and 3 cities before competitors, establishing strong brand recognition.
⇒ Digital Innovation: Early adoption of mobile ordering and payments, plus creative social media campaigns, helped KFC stay relevant to young consumers.
⇒ Cultural Sensitivity: KFC positioned itself as a respectable dining option, not just a fast-food joint, aligning with Chinese values around meals as social experiences.

Lessons: KFC's success demonstrates the power of localization, first-mover advantage, and digital adaptation in the Chinese market.

Case Study 2: Auntie Anne's - The Cautionary Tale

Auntie Anne's, the American pretzel chain, entered China in 2008 with high hopes. By 2017, it had closed all its stores in mainland China.

Factors contributing to its failure:

⇒ Product Mismatch: Pretzels were unfamiliar to most Chinese consumers and didn't align with local snacking preferences.
⇒ Pricing Strategy: Positioned as a premium product, Auntie Anne's pretzels were perceived as overpriced for a simple snack.
⇒ Location Strategy: Focusing on shopping mall locations limited exposure and foot traffic.
⇒ Lack of Localization: Unlike successful foreign brands, Auntie Anne's didn't sufficiently adapt its menu or marketing to local tastes.

Lessons: Auntie Anne's experience highlights the risks of insufficient market research, the importance of product-market fit, and the necessity of adapting to local consumer behaviours.

The Road Ahead

As we've seen, franchising in China offers immense potential but requires careful navigation. Success in this dynamic market demands a deep understanding of local culture, consumer behaviour, and regulatory landscape, coupled with the flexibility to adapt and innovate.

For franchises eyeing the Chinese market, the key takeaways are:

⇒ Localization is non-negotiable but must be balanced with brand integrity.
⇒ Digital integration is crucial for reaching and engaging Chinese consumers.
⇒ Regulatory compliance requires ongoing attention and local expertise.
⇒ Patience and long-term commitment are essential; overnight success is rare.
⇒ Continuous innovation and adaptation are necessary to stay relevant in this fast-moving market.

As we move forward in our exploration of Asian markets, remember that China, with its unique blend of ancient tradition and hyper-modernity, sets the stage for many of the opportunities and challenges we'll encounter across the region. The lessons learned here will serve as valuable guideposts as we venture into other Asian franchise frontiers.

In the world of franchising, China is not just a market; it's a masterclass in adaptation, innovation, and perseverance. Those who can learn these lessons stand to reap rich rewards in the Middle Kingdom and beyond.

South Korea

Market Overview

The Peninsula of Possibilities

South Korea, often referred to as the "Miracle on the Han River" due to its rapid economic development, has become a hotbed for franchising. Key market statistics include:

- ⇒ Population: Approximately 51 million (2021)
- ⇒ GDP: $1.65 trillion (2021)
- ⇒ GDP per capita: $31,489 (2021)
- ⇒ Urbanization rate: 81.4% (2021)

The franchise industry in South Korea has seen remarkable growth:

- ⇒ Number of franchise brands: Over 6,000 (2021)
- ⇒ Number of franchise outlets: Approximately 230,000 (2021)
- ⇒ Franchise industry contribution to GDP: About 7% (2021)

Key sectors for franchising include:

- ⇒ Food and Beverage: From Korean BBQ to bubble tea chains
- ⇒ Retail: Fashion, cosmetics, and convenience stores
- ⇒ Services: Education, beauty, and fitness
- ⇒ Entertainment: Karaoke rooms, PC bangs (internet cafes)

The Korean consumer is sophisticated, tech-savvy, and trend-conscious. There's a strong emphasis on quality, innovation, and unique experiences. The "ppalli-ppalli" (hurry-hurry) culture influences consumer behaviour, with a preference for quick service and instant gratification.

Regulatory Environment

Navigating the Korean Regulatory Landscape

South Korea has a well-developed regulatory framework for franchising, aimed at promoting fair business practices and protecting franchisees. The primary legislation governing franchising is the Fair Transactions in Franchise Business Act (Franchise Act).

Key regulatory aspects include:

⇒ Disclosure Requirements: Franchisors must provide a disclosure document to potential franchisees at least 14 days before signing a franchise agreement or receiving any payments.
⇒ Registration: Franchise disclosure documents must be registered with the Korea Fair Trade Commission (KFTC) before being used.
⇒ Cooling-off Period: Franchisees have a 14-day cooling-off period after signing the franchise agreement during which they can cancel without penalty.
⇒ Minimum Term: Franchise agreements must have a minimum term of one year.
⇒ Good Faith Obligation: Both franchisor and franchisee are required to deal with each other in good faith.
⇒ Restrictions on Unfair Trade Practices: The KFTC actively monitors and regulates unfair practices in franchising.
⇒ Trademark Registration: Franchisors must have their trademarks registered in Korea before franchising.

Recent regulatory trends include increased protection for franchisees and stricter enforcement of fair-trade practices.

Opportunities

The Land of Opportunity

South Korea offers numerous opportunities for franchising:

⇒ Tech-Savvy Market: Korea's advanced digital infrastructure allows for innovative franchise concepts, especially those leveraging mobile technology and AI.

⇒ Trend-Setting Culture: Korea's cultural influence (Hallyu or Korean Wave) creates opportunities for franchises to tap into global trends originating in Korea.

⇒ Quality-Conscious Consumers: There's a growing market for premium and luxury franchise concepts, particularly in fashion and F&B.

⇒ Overseas Expansion: Many Korean franchises are successfully expanding internationally, riding on the popularity of Korean culture.

⇒ Aging Population: This demographic shift is creating opportunities in healthcare, senior care, and related services.

⇒ Work-Life Balance Trend: Increasing emphasis on leisure and personal time is boosting franchises in fitness, hobby-related retail, and experiential dining.

⇒ Sustainability Focus: Growing environmental awareness is creating opportunities for eco-friendly and sustainable franchise concepts.

Challenges

Hurdles on the Korean Peninsula

Despite the opportunities, franchising in South Korea comes with its share of challenges:

⇒ Market Saturation: Many sectors, especially in F&B, are highly saturated, making differentiation crucial.

⇒ Fast-Changing Consumer Trends: The "ppalli-ppalli" culture extends to business, with trends changing rapidly, requiring franchises to constantly innovate.

⇒ High Rental Costs: Especially in prime locations in major cities, high rents can squeeze profit margins.

⇒ Labour Costs: Rising minimum wages and strict labour laws can increase operational costs.

⇒ Intense Competition: Both from domestic and international brands, requiring significant marketing investment to stand out.

⇒ Cultural Nuances: Misunderstanding Korean business culture and consumer preferences can lead to costly mistakes.

⇒ Regulatory Compliance: Keeping up with evolving regulations and ensuring compliance can be challenging, especially for foreign franchisors.

⇒ Economic Dependence on Chaebols: The dominance of large conglomerates can make it difficult for smaller franchises to compete in certain sectors.

Case Studies

Tales from the Land of Morning Calm

Let's examine two contrasting case studies to illustrate the realities of franchising in South Korea:

Case Study 1: Paris Baguette - The Global Korean Success Story

Paris Baguette, founded in 1988, has become one of South Korea's most successful franchise exports. Despite its French-inspired name, it's a homegrown Korean brand that has successfully expanded both domestically and internationally.

Keys to success:

⇒ Localization with a Global Twist: While maintaining a European bakery image, Paris Baguette adapted its offerings to Korean tastes, creating unique items like sweet red bean bread alongside traditional pastries.

⇒ Quality Focus: Emphasis on fresh, high-quality ingredients resonated with Korean consumers' increasing health consciousness.

⇒ Strategic Expansion: Careful selection of prime locations and a mix of company-owned and franchised stores enabled rapid but controlled growth.
⇒ International Ambitions: Expanded into other Asian markets and the US, positioning itself as a premium Asian bakery brand.
⇒ Digital Integration: Early adoption of mobile ordering and payment systems, plus creative use of social media marketing.

Lessons: Paris Baguette's success demonstrates the power of blending local tastes with global appeal, maintaining consistent quality, and leveraging technology in the Korean market.

Case Study 2: Twosome Place - Adaptation and Rebranding

Twosome Place, originally a joint venture between Korean company CJ Foodville and Starbucks, has undergone significant changes since its inception in 2002.

Key developments:

⇒ Initial Success: Positioned as a premium coffee and dessert cafe, it quickly gained popularity among young Koreans.
⇒ Ownership Changes: CJ Foodville bought out Starbucks' share in 2007, then sold the brand to a private equity firm in 2020.
⇒ Rebranding Efforts: Faced with intense competition in the cafe market, Twosome Place has continually evolved its concept, moving towards a more diverse menu and lifestyle-oriented positioning.
⇒ Challenges: Despite its efforts, Twosome Place has faced difficulties in differentiating itself in the saturated Korean cafe market.

Lessons: Twosome Place's journey highlights the challenges of maintaining relevance in Korea's fast-changing market, the importance of clear brand positioning, and the potential pitfalls of operating in a highly competitive sector.

The Path Forward

Franchising in South Korea offers a unique blend of opportunities and challenges. Success in this dynamic market requires:

⇒ Deep understanding of Korean consumer behaviour and cultural nuances
⇒ Continuous innovation to stay ahead of rapidly changing trends
⇒ Strong digital strategy, leveraging Korea's advanced tech infrastructure
⇒ Careful navigation of the regulatory environment
⇒ Quality-focused approach to meet high consumer expectations
⇒ Flexibility to adapt to market changes while maintaining brand integrity

As we continue our journey through Asian franchising landscapes, South Korea stands out as a market where cutting-edge modernity meets traditional values. It's a market that rewards innovation, quality, and cultural sensitivity, offering valuable lessons for franchise operations across Asia and beyond.

In the vibrant world of Korean franchising, success is not just about selling a product or service – it's about becoming part of the fast-paced, trend-setting Korean lifestyle. Those who can achieve this stand to thrive not just in Korea, but potentially on the global stage, riding the wave of Korean cultural influence.

Japan

Market Overview

The Harmony of Tradition and Innovation

Japan, the world's third-largest economy, presents a mature yet still evolving franchise landscape:

⇒ Population: Approximately 125 million (2021)
⇒ GDP: $5.06 trillion (2021)
⇒ GDP per capita: $40,193 (2021)
⇒ Urbanization rate: 91.8% (2021)

The franchise industry in Japan is well-established:

⇒ Number of franchise chains: Over 1,300 (2021)
⇒ Number of franchise outlets: Approximately 260,000 (2021)
⇒ Franchise industry annual sales: ¥25.5 trillion (about $230 billion) (2021)

Key sectors for franchising include:

⇒ Convenience Stores (Konbini): A cornerstone of Japanese daily life
⇒ Food and Beverage: From ramen shops to coffee chains
⇒ Retail: Particularly in fashion, electronics, and home goods
⇒ Services: Including cleaning, fitness, and beauty services
⇒ Education: Cram schools (juku) and language schools

Japanese consumers are known for their high expectations of quality and service. There's a strong emphasis on attention to detail, cleanliness, and omotenashi (wholehearted hospitality). The aging population and increasing number of single-person households are shaping consumer trends, with growing demand for convenience and health-oriented products and services.

Regulatory Environment

Navigating the Japanese Regulatory Landscape

Japan's franchise industry is regulated primarily by the Medium and Small Retail Commerce Promotion Act, which includes specific provisions for franchise businesses. The Japan Fair Trade Commission (JFTC) oversees the implementation of these regulations.

Key regulatory aspects include:

⇒ Disclosure Requirements: Franchisors must provide a detailed disclosure document to potential franchisees at least 7 days before signing a contract or receiving any payments.

⇒ No Registration Requirement: Unlike many countries, Japan does not require franchisors to register with a government agency.

⇒ Cooling-off Period: While not mandatory, many franchise agreements include a cooling-off period allowing franchisees to cancel within a specified timeframe.

⇒ Anti-Monopoly Act: This law prohibits unfair trade practices, which can apply to certain franchisor-franchisee relationships.

⇒ Trademark Registration: Franchisors must have their trademarks registered in Japan before franchising.

⇒ Personal Information Protection: The Act on the Protection of Personal Information applies to franchise businesses handling customer data.

Recent regulatory trends include increased focus on fair trade practices and consumer protection.

Opportunities

The Rising Sun of Opportunity

Japan offers several unique opportunities for franchising:

⇒ Aging Population: This demographic shift creates opportunities in healthcare, senior care, and related services.

⇒ Tourism Growth: Pre-pandemic tourism boom (expected to recover) creates opportunities for hospitality and retail franchises.

⇒ Work-Style Reform: Government initiatives to improve work-life balance are boosting demand for convenience and time-saving services.

⇒ Technology Adoption: Japan's embrace of technology opens doors for innovative, tech-driven franchise concepts.

⇒ Quality-Conscious Market: High appreciation for quality products and services allows premium franchise concepts to thrive.

⇒ Convenience Culture: The busy lifestyle of urban Japanese creates constant demand for convenient solutions.

⇒ Overseas Expansion: Many Japanese franchises are successfully expanding internationally, particularly in Asia.

Challenges

Scaling Mount Fuji

Franchising in Japan comes with its unique set of challenges:

⇒ Aging and Shrinking Population: While creating some opportunities, this also leads to a shrinking domestic market and labour shortages.

⇒ High Operating Costs: Real estate, labour, and material costs in Japan are among the highest globally.

⇒ Complex Business Culture: Understanding and navigating Japanese business etiquette and decision-making processes can be challenging for foreign franchisors.

⇒ Consumer Expectations: Japanese consumers have extremely high standards for quality and service, requiring meticulous attention to detail.

⇒ Market Saturation: Many sectors, especially in retail and food service, are highly saturated.

⇒ Localization Needs: Products and services often need significant adaptation to suit Japanese tastes and customs.

⇒ Economic Stagnation: Japan's economy has experienced prolonged periods of slow growth, affecting consumer spending.

⇒ Natural Disaster Risk: Japan's geographical location makes it prone to earthquakes and tsunamis, necessitating robust risk management strategies.

Case Studies

Tales from the Land of the Rising Sun

Let's examine two contrasting case studies to illustrate the realities of franchising in Japan:

Case Study 1: 7-Eleven Japan - The Konbini King

7-Eleven, originally an American brand, has become an integral part of Japanese daily life, with over 20,000 stores nationwide.

Keys to success:

⇒ Localization: Adapted product offerings to Japanese tastes, including ready-to-eat meals, seasonal items, and services like bill payment and package delivery.

⇒ Innovation: Pioneered the concept of convenience stores as multi-service hubs.

⇒ Supply Chain Excellence: Developed a highly efficient, just-in-time inventory system.
⇒ Technology Integration: Early adoption of advanced POS systems and data analytics to optimize product selection and inventory.
⇒ Quality Focus: Maintained high standards of product quality and store cleanliness, aligning with Japanese consumer expectations.

Lessons: 7-Eleven's success in Japan demonstrates the power of thorough localization, continuous innovation, and leveraging technology to meet evolving consumer needs.

Case Study 2: Yoshinoya - Domestic Success, International Challenges

Yoshinoya, a Japanese fast-food chain famous for its beef bowls, has had a mixed record of international expansion.

Key developments:

⇒ Domestic Strength: Strong brand recognition and loyal customer base in Japan.
⇒ International Expansion: Successful in some Asian markets but faced challenges in others, including the United States.
⇒ Adaptation Struggles: In some international markets, struggled to adapt its menu and service style to local preferences.
⇒ Price Point Challenges: Positioning as a low-cost option in Japan didn't always translate well to other markets.
⇒ Recent Innovations: Responding to changing domestic market conditions by introducing new menu items and exploring vegetarian options.

Lessons: Yoshinoya's journey highlights the challenges of translating domestic success to international markets and the importance of adapting not just products, but also brand positioning and operational models to local contexts.

The Way of the Samurai Franchisor

Success in Japan's franchise market requires a blend of respect for tradition and embrace of innovation:

⇒ Impeccable quality and service are non-negotiable
⇒ Deep understanding of Japanese consumer behaviour and business culture is crucial
⇒ Continuous innovation and adaptation are necessary to stay relevant
⇒ Technology integration can provide a significant competitive advantage
⇒ Patience and long-term commitment are essential; building trust takes time in Japan
⇒ Careful balance between maintaining global brand identity and localizing for Japanese tastes

As we continue our exploration of Asian franchising landscapes, Japan stands out as a market where attention to detail, quality, and customer service reach their zenith. It's a challenging market that demands excellence but rewards those who can deliver with loyal customers and potentially, a strong base for regional expansion.

In the land of the rising sun, franchising success is not just about selling a product or service – it's about becoming a seamless part of the Japanese way of life, respecting traditions while embracing the future. Those who can achieve this delicate balance may find themselves not just succeeding in Japan but setting new global standards for franchise excellence.

Taiwan

Market Overview

The Heart of Asia's Economic Miracle

Taiwan, often referred to as the "Beautiful Island," has transformed itself into an economic powerhouse:

⇒ Population: Approximately 23.5 million (2021)
⇒ GDP: $668.51 billion (2021)
⇒ GDP per capita: $28,371 (2021)
⇒ Urbanization rate: 79.1% (2021)

The franchise industry in Taiwan has seen steady growth:

⇒ Number of franchise brands: Over 2,500 (2021)
⇒ Number of franchise outlets: Approximately 120,000 (2021)
⇒ Franchise industry contribution to GDP: About 5% (2021)

Key sectors for franchising include:

⇒ Food and Beverage: From bubble tea shops to hot pot restaurants
⇒ Retail: Convenience stores, fashion, and specialty goods
⇒ Services: Education, beauty, and fitness
⇒ Healthcare: Pharmacies and wellness centres

Taiwanese consumers are known for their openness to new concepts, love for convenience, and appreciation for value. There's a strong emphasis on food culture, with eating out being a significant part of daily life. The rise of social media has also influenced consumer behaviour, with "Instagrammable" experiences becoming increasingly important.

Regulatory Environment

Navigating Taiwan's Regulatory Waters

Taiwan has a relatively open regulatory environment for franchising, with no specific franchise law. Instead, franchising is governed by various existing laws and regulations.

Key regulatory aspects include:

⇒ No Specific Franchise Law: Franchise relationships are primarily governed by general commercial laws and the Civil Code.
⇒ No Mandatory Disclosure: Unlike many countries, Taiwan does not have mandatory pre-contractual disclosure requirements for franchisors.
⇒ Fair Trade Act: This law prohibits unfair competition and deceptive practices, which can apply to franchise relationships.
⇒ Consumer Protection Act: This can apply to franchise agreements if the franchisee is considered a consumer.
⇒ Trademark Registration: Franchisors must register their trademarks in Taiwan before franchising.
⇒ Personal Data Protection Act: This law governs the collection and use of personal data, which is relevant for franchise operations.

Recent regulatory trends include increased focus on fair trade practices and consumer protection, particularly in the food and beverage sector.

Opportunities

The Pearl of Asia's Franchise Market

Taiwan offers numerous opportunities for franchising:

⇒ Tech-Savvy Market: Taiwan's advanced technology sector creates opportunities for innovative, tech-driven franchise concepts.

⇒ Growing Health Consciousness: Increasing demand for health and wellness products and services.

⇒ Aging Population: This demographic shift is creating opportunities in healthcare and elderly care services.

⇒ Tourism Growth: Pre-pandemic tourism boom (expected to recover) creates opportunities for hospitality and retail franchises.

⇒ Regional Expansion Hub: Taiwan's strategic location and cultural ties make it an excellent base for expansion into other Asian markets.

⇒ Strong Food Culture: Constant demand for new and innovative food concepts.

⇒ E-commerce Integration: Growing opportunities for franchises that can effectively integrate online and offline experiences.

Challenges

Navigating the Strait

Despite the opportunities, franchising in Taiwan comes with its share of challenges:

⇒ Market Saturation: Many sectors, especially in F&B, are highly competitive and saturated.

⇒ Small Domestic Market: With a population of only 23.5 million, the market can be limiting for some concepts.

⇒ Cultural Nuances: Understanding and adapting to local tastes and business practices can be challenging for foreign franchisors.

⇒ Political Uncertainty: Taiwan's complex relationship with China can create business uncertainties.

⇒ Labor Issues: Rising labour costs and difficulties in recruiting and retaining staff, especially in the service sector.

⇒ Intellectual Property Protection: While improving, enforcement of IP rights can still be a concern.

⇒ Language Barrier: While English is widely spoken in business circles, proficiency in Mandarin is often necessary for day-to-day operations.

Case Studies

Tales from Formosa

Let's examine two contrasting case studies to illustrate the realities of franchising in Taiwan:

Case Study 1: 85°C Bakery Cafe - From Taiwan to the World

85°C Bakery Cafe, founded in 2004 in Taiwan, has become a global phenomenon, often referred to as the "Starbucks of Taiwan."

Keys to success:

⇒ Quality at Affordable Prices: Offered high-quality baked goods and coffee at competitive prices.

⇒ Innovation: Regularly introduced new products, including the sea salt coffee that became a signature item.

⇒ Experiential Retail: Created a unique in-store experience with open bakeries and self-service format.

⇒ Global Expansion: Successfully expanded to China, Australia, and the United States, adapting its offerings to local tastes.

⇒ Brand Positioning: Positioned itself as an upscale yet affordable option, appealing to a wide range of consumers.

Lessons: 85°C's success demonstrates the potential for Taiwanese brands to go global by offering innovative products, creating unique experiences, and adapting to local markets while maintaining core brand values.

Case Study 2: Quickly - Rapid Expansion and Contraction

Quickly, a Taiwanese bubble tea franchise, experienced rapid global expansion followed by significant contraction.

Key developments:

⇒ Rapid Growth: Expanded to over 2,000 locations worldwide in the early 2000s.

⇒ Overexpansion Issues: Faced challenges maintaining quality and consistency across its vast network.

⇒ Brand Dilution: The rapid expansion led to inconsistent brand experiences in different markets.

⇒ Contraction: Many international locations closed, particularly in the United States.

⇒ Domestic Resilience: Despite international challenges, maintained a strong presence in Taiwan.

⇒ Recent Efforts: Focusing on improving product quality and store operations to rebuild brand reputation.

Lessons: Quickly's journey highlights the risks of rapid expansion without adequate quality control and the importance of maintaining brand consistency across markets. It also demonstrates the resilience of strong domestic market presence.

The Taiwanese Way

Success in Taiwan's franchise market requires a blend of innovation, adaptability, and respect for local culture:

⇒ Focus on food innovation and quality, given the importance of food culture in Taiwan

⇒ Embrace technology and social media to engage with tech-savvy Taiwanese consumers

⇒ Develop strong relationships with local partners to navigate cultural and business nuances

⇒ Balance standardization with localization to meet Taiwanese consumer preferences

⇒ Consider Taiwan as a potential base for regional expansion, leveraging its strategic location and business-friendly environment

⇒ Invest in staff training and retention to maintain service quality in a competitive labour market

As we continue our journey through Asian franchising landscapes, Taiwan stands out as a market where innovation meets tradition, and local success can be a springboard to regional or even global expansion. It's a market that rewards creativity, quality, and adaptability, offering valuable lessons for franchise operations across Asia and beyond.

In the vibrant world of Taiwanese franchising, success is not just about selling a product or service – it's about becoming part of the island's dynamic culture and everyday life. Those who can achieve this stand to thrive not just in Taiwan, but potentially across the Asia-Pacific region and beyond, riding the wave of Taiwan's economic influence and innovative spirit.

Vietnam

Market Overview

A Symphony of Growth and Tradition

Vietnam has emerged as one of Southeast Asia's fastest-growing economies:

⇒ Population: Approximately 98 million (2021)
⇒ GDP: $362.64 billion (2021)
⇒ GDP per capita: $3,694 (2021)
⇒ Urbanization rate: 37.3% (2021)

The franchise industry in Vietnam is relatively young but growing rapidly:

⇒ Number of foreign franchise brands: Over 200 (2021)
⇒ Number of domestic franchise brands: Approximately 100 (2021)
⇒ Annual growth rate of franchise industry: 15-20% (pre-pandemic)

Key sectors for franchising include:

⇒ Food and Beverage: From fast food to coffee shops
⇒ Retail: Fashion, convenience stores, and specialty goods
⇒ Education: Language schools and tutoring centres
⇒ Services: Beauty, spa, and fitness

Vietnamese consumers are characterized by their youth (median age of 32.5 years), increasing urbanization, and growing middle class. There's a strong appetite for foreign brands, seen as symbols of quality and status. However, there's also a deep appreciation for local flavours and traditions, necessitating a balanced approach for franchisors.

Regulatory Environment

Navigating the Regulatory Waterways of Vietnam

Vietnam has a specific legal framework for franchising, which has been evolving since its introduction in 2006:

> ⇒ Commercial Law and Decree 35: These form the primary legal basis for franchising in Vietnam.
> ⇒ Disclosure Requirements: Franchisors must provide a disclosure document to potential franchisees at least 15 working days before signing a franchise agreement.
> ⇒ Registration Requirement: Foreign franchisors must register their franchise with the Ministry of Industry and Trade before operating in Vietnam.
> ⇒ Trademark Registration: Franchisors must have their trademarks registered in Vietnam before franchising.
> ⇒ Language Requirement: Franchise agreements must be in Vietnamese, though bilingual versions are allowed.
> ⇒ Sub-franchising: Sub-franchising is permitted, but the sub-franchisor must be a Vietnamese entity.

Recent regulatory trends include increased focus on consumer protection and food safety, particularly relevant for F&B franchises.

Opportunities

The Golden Dragon's Treasures

Vietnam offers several exciting opportunities for franchising:

> ⇒ Young Population: With over 60% of the population under 35, there's a large, receptive market for new concepts.
> ⇒ Rising Middle Class: The rapidly growing middle class is driving demand for quality products and services.

⇒ Urbanization: Increasing urbanization is creating demand for convenience and modern retail concepts.

⇒ Digital Adoption: High smartphone penetration and internet usage create opportunities for tech-integrated franchise models.

⇒ Tourism Growth: Pre-pandemic tourism boom (expected to recover) creates opportunities in hospitality and retail.

⇒ Government Support: The government is actively promoting foreign investment and franchising.

⇒ Regional Expansion Hub: Vietnam's strategic location makes it a potential base for expansion into other Southeast Asian markets.

Challenges

Crossing the Mekong

Despite the opportunities, franchising in Vietnam comes with its unique set of challenges:

⇒ Complex Bureaucracy: Navigating government regulations and procedures can be time-consuming and complex.

⇒ Cultural Differences: Understanding and adapting to local tastes and business practices can be challenging for foreign franchisors.

⇒ Intellectual Property Protection: While improving, enforcement of IP rights can still be a concern.

⇒ Finding Qualified Franchisees: The concept of franchising is still relatively new, and finding experienced, well-capitalized franchisees can be difficult.

⇒ Supply Chain Issues: Developing reliable local supply chains can be challenging, especially for food franchises.

⇒ Competition: The market is becoming increasingly competitive, with both foreign and domestic brands vying for market share.

⇒ Economic Disparities: Significant income differences between major cities and rural areas necessitate careful market selection.

Case Studies

Tales from the Land of the Ascending Dragon

Let's examine two contrasting case studies to illustrate the realities of franchising in Vietnam:

Case Study 1: Highlands Coffee - Local Brand Goes Big

Highlands Coffee, founded in Vietnam in 1999, has grown to become one of the country's largest coffee shop chains.

Keys to success:

⇒ Local Roots: Leveraged its Vietnamese origin to appeal to local pride and tastes.
⇒ Adaptation: Successfully blended international coffee shop concepts with local flavours and preferences.
⇒ Strategic Expansion: Focused on prime locations in major cities before expanding to smaller markets.
⇒ Menu Innovation: Regularly introduced new products combining international trends with local tastes.
⇒ Brand Positioning: Positioned itself as a modern, aspirational brand for Vietnam's growing middle class.

Lessons: Highlands Coffee's success demonstrates the potential for local brands to thrive by combining international concepts with deep local market understanding.

Case Study 2: Circle K - International Convenience in Vietnam

Circle K, an international convenience store chain, has rapidly expanded in Vietnam since entering the market in 2008.

Key developments:

⇒ Rapid Expansion: Grew to over 400 stores across major cities in Vietnam.
⇒ Localization: Adapted product offerings to local tastes while maintaining global brand standards.
⇒ 24/7 Operations: Introduced the concept of 24-hour convenience stores, meeting the needs of Vietnam's young, urban population.
⇒ Tech Integration: Implemented modern POS systems and introduced mobile payment options.
⇒ Challenges: Faced intense competition from local convenience store chains and traditional markets.
⇒ Recent Efforts: Focusing on expanding fresh food offerings and enhancing in-store experiences to differentiate from competitors.

Lessons: Circle K's journey highlights the importance of balancing global brand standards with local market adaptation, and the potential for introducing new retail concepts in a rapidly developing market.

The Vietnamese Way

Success in Vietnam's franchise market requires a blend of innovation, cultural sensitivity, and adaptability:

⇒ Prioritize relationship-building with local partners and government officials
⇒ Invest time in understanding local consumer preferences and adapting offerings accordingly
⇒ Be prepared for a long-term commitment, as building brand awareness and trust takes time
⇒ Develop robust training programs to ensure consistent quality across franchise outlets
⇒ Consider a phased approach to expansion, starting in major cities before moving to smaller markets

⇒ Embrace digital technologies to engage with Vietnam's tech-savvy young consumers

As we navigate through the diverse franchising landscapes of Asia, Vietnam emerges as a market of immense potential, characterized by its youthful energy, rapid economic growth, and evolving consumer tastes. It's a market that rewards those who can skilfully blend international standards with local flavours, offering valuable lessons for franchise operations across the region.

In the dynamic world of Vietnamese franchising, success is not just about introducing a proven concept – it's about becoming part of Vietnam's exciting journey of economic transformation. Those who can achieve this stand to thrive not just in Vietnam, but potentially across Southeast Asia, riding the wave of Vietnam's growing economic influence and entrepreneurial spirit.

Thailand

Market Overview

A Tapestry of Tradition and Modernity

Thailand has established itself as a key player in Southeast Asia's economy:

⇒ Population: Approximately 69.8 million (2021)
⇒ GDP: $505.9 billion (2021)
⇒ GDP per capita: $7,233 (2021)
⇒ Urbanization rate: 51.4% (2021)

The franchise industry in Thailand has seen steady growth:

⇒ Number of franchise brands: Over 550 (2021)
⇒ Number of franchise outlets: Approximately 75,000 (2021)
⇒ Franchise industry contribution to GDP: About 3% (2021)

Key sectors for franchising include:

⇒ Food and Beverage: From quick-service restaurants to bubble tea shops
⇒ Retail: Convenience stores, fashion, and specialty goods
⇒ Services: Education, beauty, and wellness
⇒ Hospitality: Hotels and tourism-related services

Thai consumers are known for their brand consciousness, love for convenience, and openness to new concepts. There's a strong emphasis on food culture, with eating out being a significant part of daily life. The rise of social media has also influenced consumer behaviour, with "shareable" experiences becoming increasingly important.

Regulatory Environment

Navigating the Golden Land's Legal Landscape

Thailand has a relatively open regulatory environment for franchising, with no specific franchise law. Instead, franchising is governed by various existing laws and regulations.

Key regulatory aspects include:

⇒ No Specific Franchise Law: Franchise relationships are primarily governed by general commercial laws and the Civil and Commercial Code.
⇒ Trade Competition Act: This law regulates fair competition and can apply to franchise relationships.
⇒ Trademark Registration: Franchisors must register their trademarks in Thailand before franchising.
⇒ Foreign Business Act: This law restricts foreign ownership in certain business sectors, which can affect foreign franchisors.
⇒ Personal Data Protection Act: Implemented in 2022, this law governs the collection and use of personal data, which is relevant for franchise operations.
⇒ No Mandatory Disclosure: Unlike some countries, Thailand does not have mandatory pre-contractual disclosure requirements for franchisors.

Recent regulatory trends include increased focus on data protection and consumer rights, particularly in the digital space.

Opportunities

The Land of Golden Opportunities

Thailand offers numerous opportunities for franchising:

⇒ Growing Middle Class: An expanding middle class with increasing disposable income creates demand for quality products and services.

⇒ Tourism Industry: Thailand's strong tourism sector (expected to recover post-pandemic) creates opportunities for hospitality and retail franchises.

⇒ Digital Adoption: High smartphone penetration and internet usage create opportunities for tech-integrated franchise models.

⇒ Regional Hub: Thailand's strategic location and developed infrastructure make it an excellent base for expansion into other Southeast Asian markets.

⇒ Government Support: The Thai government has been supportive of SMEs and franchise businesses.

⇒ Urbanization: Increasing urbanization is driving demand for convenience and modern retail concepts.

⇒ Health and Wellness Trend: Growing health consciousness creates opportunities in fitness, healthy food, and wellness sectors.

Challenges

Navigating the Tropical Terrain

Despite the opportunities, franchising in Thailand comes with its share of challenges:

⇒ Cultural Nuances: Understanding and adapting to local tastes and business practices can be challenging for foreign franchisors.

⇒ Competition: The market is becoming increasingly saturated in certain sectors, particularly F&B.

⇒ Political Instability: Periodic political unrest can create uncertainty for businesses.

⇒ Intellectual Property Protection: While improving, enforcement of IP rights can still be a concern.

⇒ Language Barrier: While English is widely used in business, proficiency in Thai is often necessary for day-to-day operations.

⇒ Economic Disparities: Significant income differences between Bangkok and other regions necessitate careful market selection.

⇒ Labour Issues: Finding and retaining skilled labour can be challenging, particularly in the service sector.

Case Studies

Tales from the Kingdom

Let's examine two contrasting case studies to illustrate the realities of franchising in Thailand:

Case Study 1: Café Amazon - From Gas Stations to Global Brand

Café Amazon, a coffee shop chain owned by Thailand's state oil company PTT, has become one of the country's most successful franchise stories.

Keys to success:

⇒ Strategic Locations: Initially leveraged PTT's extensive network of gas stations for rapid expansion.

⇒ Local Flavours: Offered a menu that catered to Thai tastes while maintaining international coffee shop standards.

⇒ Affordable Pricing: Positioned itself as a quality yet affordable option, appealing to a wide range of consumers.

⇒ Brand Identity: Developed a strong, recognizable brand with a distinct "green" theme.

⇒ International Expansion: Successfully expanded to neighbouring countries and beyond, adapting its model to local markets.

Lessons: Café Amazon's success demonstrates the potential for locally developed brands to achieve national and international success by leveraging existing networks and understanding local consumer preferences.

Case Study 2: Tesco Lotus - Adapting to Local Regulations

Tesco, the British retail giant, entered Thailand in 1998 through a joint venture, creating Tesco Lotus.

Key developments:

⇒ Rapid Growth: Expanded to become one of Thailand's largest retailers.
⇒ Format Diversification: Developed various store formats to cater to different market segments.
⇒ Local Sourcing: Established strong relationships with local suppliers.
⇒ Regulatory Challenges: Faced scrutiny under Thailand's retail regulations, leading to restrictions on further expansion of large-format stores.
⇒ Adaptation: Shifted focus to smaller format stores and e-commerce to continue growth.
⇒ Ownership Change: In 2020, Tesco sold its Thai operations to a local conglomerate, marking a significant shift in the retail landscape.

Lessons: Tesco Lotus's journey highlights the importance of adapting to local regulations and market conditions, as well as the potential for successful exits in the Thai market.

The Thai Way

Success in Thailand's franchise market requires a blend of innovation, cultural sensitivity, and adaptability:

⇒ Invest time in understanding local consumer preferences and adapting offerings accordingly

⇒ Develop strong relationships with local partners to navigate cultural and business nuances

⇒ Embrace digital technologies to engage with Thailand's tech-savvy consumers

⇒ Consider a multi-format approach to cater to different market segments

⇒ Be prepared for a long-term commitment, as building brand loyalty takes time in Thailand

⇒ Balance standardization with localization to meet Thai consumer expectations

As we continue our journey through Asian franchising landscapes, Thailand stands out as a market where tradition meets modernity, and local tastes blend with global trends. It's a market that rewards creativity, quality, and cultural sensitivity, offering valuable lessons for franchise operations across Southeast Asia and beyond.

In the vibrant world of Thai franchising, success is not just about selling a product or service – it's about becoming part of the country's rich tapestry of experiences and flavours. Those who can achieve this stand to thrive not just in Thailand, but potentially across the region, leveraging Thailand's strategic position and consumer-driven economy.

Malaysia

Market Overview

A Tapestry of Cultures and Commerce

Malaysia has established itself as a key player in Southeast Asia's economy:

⇒ Population: Approximately 32.7 million (2021)
⇒ GDP: $372.7 billion (2021)
⇒ GDP per capita: $11,371 (2021)
⇒ Urbanization rate: 77.2% (2021)

The franchise industry in Malaysia has seen robust growth:

⇒ Number of franchise brands: Over 900 (2021)
⇒ Number of franchise outlets: Approximately 13,000 (2021)
⇒ Franchise industry contribution to GDP: About 4% (2021)

Key sectors for franchising include:

⇒ Food and Beverage: From fast food to local cuisine concepts
⇒ Retail: Fashion, convenience stores, and specialty goods
⇒ Services: Education, beauty, and wellness
⇒ Automotive: Car maintenance and repair services

Malaysian consumers are characterized by their cultural diversity, tech-savviness, and growing middle class. There's a strong appetite for both international and local brands, with an increasing emphasis on halal products and services to cater to the country's Muslim majority.

Regulatory Environment

Navigating the Regulatory Landscape of Malaysia

Malaysia has a well-developed regulatory framework for franchising:

⇒ Franchise Act 1998: This act governs franchise relationships and operations in Malaysia.
⇒ Franchise Registry: All franchisors must register with the Franchise Registry under the Ministry of Domestic Trade and Consumer Affairs before operating in Malaysia.
⇒ Disclosure Requirements: Franchisors must provide a disclosure document to potential franchisees at least 10 days before signing a franchise agreement.
⇒ Halal Certification: For food and beverage franchises, halal certification is often necessary to cater to the Muslim population.
⇒ Bumiputera Ownership: Some sectors may require a certain percentage of Bumiputera (indigenous Malay) ownership.
⇒ Trademark Registration: Franchisors must register their trademarks in Malaysia before franchising.

Recent regulatory trends include increased focus on digital businesses and e-commerce, as well as efforts to promote local franchise brands internationally.

Opportunities

The Land of Opportunity

Malaysia offers several exciting opportunities for franchising:

⇒ Growing Middle Class: An expanding middle class with increasing disposable income creates demand for quality products and services.
⇒ Cultural Diversity: Malaysia's multi-ethnic population provides opportunities for diverse franchise concepts.

⇒ Halal Market: Malaysia's position as a global halal hub creates opportunities for halal-certified franchises.

⇒ Digital Adoption: High smartphone penetration and internet usage create opportunities for tech-integrated franchise models.

⇒ Government Support: The Malaysian government actively promotes franchising through various initiatives and support programs.

⇒ Regional Hub: Malaysia's strategic location and developed infrastructure make it an excellent base for expansion into other Southeast Asian markets.

⇒ Tourism Industry: Malaysia's strong tourism sector (expected to recover post-pandemic) creates opportunities for hospitality and retail franchises.

Challenges

Navigating the Malaysian Marketplace

Despite the opportunities, franchising in Malaysia comes with its unique set of challenges:

⇒ Cultural Sensitivities: Understanding and respecting the diverse cultural and religious norms of Malaysia's multi-ethnic population can be challenging.

⇒ Competition: The market is becoming increasingly saturated in certain sectors, particularly F&B.

⇒ Halal Requirements: For food franchises, obtaining and maintaining halal certification can be complex and time-consuming.

⇒ Economic Disparities: Significant income differences between urban and rural areas necessitate careful market selection.

⇒ Intellectual Property Protection: While improving, enforcement of IP rights can still be a concern in some cases.

⇒ Labour Issues: Finding and retaining skilled labour can be challenging, particularly in the service sector.

⇒ Currency Fluctuations: The volatility of the Malaysian Ringgit can affect profitability for international franchises.

⇒

Case Studies

Tales from the Peninsula

Let's examine two contrasting case studies to illustrate the realities of franchising in Malaysia:

Case Study 1: Old Town White Coffee - Local Flavour Goes Global

Old Town White Coffee, a Malaysian coffee shop chain, has become one of the country's most successful franchise stories.

Keys to success:

⇒ Local Roots: Leveraged its Malaysian origin and traditional white coffee recipe to appeal to local tastes.

⇒ Brand Evolution: Successfully transformed from a local coffee shop to a modern café concept.

⇒ Product Diversification: Expanded from coffee shops to packaged products sold in supermarkets.

⇒ International Expansion: Successfully expanded to other Asian markets while maintaining its Malaysian identity.

⇒ Halal Certification: Ensured all products are halal-certified, appealing to the Muslim market.

Lessons: Old Town's success demonstrates the potential for local brands to achieve national and international success by modernizing traditional concepts and adapting to diverse market needs.

Case Study 2: Subway - Adapting to Local Tastes

Subway, the American sandwich chain, has had a mixed experience in the Malaysian market.

Key developments:

⇒ Initial Success: Rapid expansion in the early 2000s, appealing to health-conscious urban consumers.

⇒ Cultural Adaptation: Introduced local flavours and ensured halal certification for all outlets.

⇒ Challenges: Faced difficulties competing with local food options and adapting to Malaysian taste preferences.

⇒ Strategic Shift: Focused on smaller format stores and increased localization of menu items.

⇒ Recent Efforts: Emphasizing digital ordering and delivery services to cater to changing consumer behaviour.

Lessons: Subway's journey in Malaysia highlights the importance of continuous adaptation to local tastes and consumer behaviour, even for well-established global brands.

The Malaysian Way

Success in Malaysia's franchise market requires a blend of cultural sensitivity, innovation, and adaptability:

⇒ Prioritize understanding and respecting Malaysia's diverse cultural and religious landscape

⇒ Invest in obtaining and maintaining halal certification for food-related franchises

⇒ Develop strong relationships with local partners to navigate regulatory and cultural nuances

⇒ Embrace digital technologies to engage with Malaysia's tech-savvy consumers

⇒ Consider a multi-format approach to cater to different market segments across urban and rural areas

⇒ Balance standardization with localization to meet diverse consumer expectations

As we continue our exploration of Asian franchising landscapes, Malaysia emerges as a market where East meets West, tradition blends with modernity, and diverse cultures converge. It's a market that rewards cultural sensitivity, quality, and innovation, offering valuable lessons for franchise operations across Southeast Asia and beyond.

In the dynamic world of Malaysian franchising, success is not just about offering a product or service – it's about becoming part of the country's rich multicultural tapestry. Those who can achieve this stand to thrive not just in Malaysia, but potentially across the region, leveraging Malaysia's strategic position as a gateway to both Islamic and non-Islamic markets in Asia.

Singapore

Market Overview

A Global City-State of Opportunities

Singapore has established itself as a global financial hub and a key player in Southeast Asia's economy:

⇒ Population: Approximately 5.7 million (2021)
⇒ GDP: $397 billion (2021)
⇒ GDP per capita: $69,649 (2021)
⇒ Urbanization rate: 100% (city-state)

The franchise industry in Singapore has seen steady growth:

⇒ Number of franchise brands: Over 700 (2021)
⇒ Number of franchise outlets: Approximately 50,000 (2021)
⇒ Franchise industry contribution to GDP: About 3% (2021)

Key sectors for franchising include:

⇒ Food and Beverage: From quick-service restaurants to fine dining concepts
⇒ Retail: Fashion, convenience stores, and specialty goods
⇒ Services: Education, beauty, and wellness
⇒ Healthcare: Medical and dental services

Singaporean consumers are known for their high purchasing power, tech-savviness, and cosmopolitan tastes. There's a strong emphasis on quality and brand reputation, with consumers willing to pay premium prices for perceived value. The city-state's multicultural population also creates demand for diverse international concepts.

Regulatory Environment

Navigating the Lion City's Business-Friendly Landscape

Singapore is renowned for its business-friendly environment, and this extends to franchising:

- ⇒ No Specific Franchise Law: Franchising is governed by general commercial laws and regulations.
- ⇒ Franchise and Licensee Association (FLA): While not a regulatory body, the FLA promotes best practices in franchising.
- ⇒ Intellectual Property Laws: Singapore has strong IP protection laws, crucial for franchising.
- ⇒ Competition Act: This law ensures fair competition practices, which can affect franchise agreements.
- ⇒ Personal Data Protection Act: Governs the collection and use of personal data, relevant for franchise operations.
- ⇒ No Mandatory Disclosure: Unlike some countries, Singapore does not have mandatory pre-contractual disclosure requirements for franchisors.

Recent regulatory trends include increased focus on data protection, cybersecurity, and fair employment practices.

Opportunities

The Garden City of Franchise Prospects

Singapore offers numerous opportunities for franchising:

- ⇒ Gateway to Southeast Asia: Singapore's strategic location and business-friendly environment make it an ideal base for regional expansion.
- ⇒ High Disposable Income: A wealthy consumer base creates opportunities for premium and luxury franchise concepts.

⇒ Digital Hub: Singapore's advanced digital infrastructure supports tech-integrated franchise models and e-commerce.

⇒ Government Support: The Singapore government offers various grants and support schemes for businesses, including franchises.

⇒ Robust Legal Framework: Strong IP protection and contract enforcement provide a secure environment for franchisors.

⇒ Multicultural Market: Singapore's diverse population allows for testing of concepts that can be scaled to other Asian markets.

⇒ Tourism Industry: Singapore's position as a major tourist destination creates opportunities for hospitality and retail franchises.

Challenges

Conquering the Lion City's Competitive Terrain

Despite its many advantages, franchising in Singapore comes with its own set of challenges:

⇒ High Costs: Singapore has one of the highest costs of living in the world, affecting operational expenses and labour costs.

⇒ Space Constraints: Limited physical space and high real estate costs can be challenging for retail and F&B franchises.

⇒ Labour Shortage: Strict foreign worker quotas and a tight labour market can make staffing difficult.

⇒ Intense Competition: The small, saturated market leads to fierce competition, especially in the F&B sector.

⇒ Changing Consumer Preferences: Singaporean consumers are known for their fickle tastes, requiring constant innovation.

⇒ Regulatory Compliance: While business-friendly, Singapore has strict regulations in areas like hygiene and employment that must be carefully navigated.
⇒ Small Domestic Market: The limited population size means that saturation can occur quickly for successful concepts.

Case Studies

Tales from the Lion City

Let's examine two contrasting case studies to illustrate the realities of franchising in Singapore:

Case Study 1: BreadTalk - From Local Bakery to Global Brand

BreadTalk, a Singaporean bakery chain, has become one of the country's most successful franchise stories.

Keys to success:

⇒ Innovation: Continuously introduced new products and concepts to keep up with changing consumer tastes.
⇒ Brand Building: Developed a strong, recognizable brand with its signature transparent kitchens.
⇒ Diversification: Expanded beyond bakeries into other F&B concepts like food courts and restaurants.
⇒ International Expansion: Successfully expanded across Asia and beyond, adapting its offerings to local tastes.
⇒ Quality Control: Maintained consistent quality across outlets through rigorous training and standardization.

Lessons: BreadTalk's success demonstrates the potential for Singaporean brands to achieve global success through innovation, strong branding, and adaptability.

Case Study 2: Wendy's - Challenges in a Competitive Market

Wendy's, the American fast-food chain, has had a challenging experience in the Singaporean market.

Key developments:

⇒ Initial Entry: Entered Singapore in the 1980s but exited in the 1990s due to fierce competition.
⇒ Re-entry: Attempted to re-enter the market in 2009.
⇒ Localization Efforts: Tried to adapt menu items to local tastes.
⇒ Challenges: Faced difficulties competing with established players and local food options.
⇒ Exit: Closed all outlets in Singapore by 2015.
⇒ Lessons Learned: The experience highlighted the importance of timing, market positioning, and sustained efforts in brand building.

Lessons: Wendy's journey in Singapore underscores the challenges even established global brands can face in Singapore's competitive market, emphasizing the need for strong differentiation and local market understanding.

The Singaporean Way

Success in Singapore's franchise market requires a blend of innovation, quality, and adaptability:

⇒ Invest in continuous innovation to stay ahead in the fast-paced market
⇒ Focus on quality and consistency to justify higher prices in the premium market
⇒ Leverage Singapore's digital infrastructure to enhance operations and customer experience
⇒ Develop a strong, unique brand identity to stand out in the crowded market

⇒ Consider using Singapore as a testbed for concepts before regional expansion

⇒ Be prepared for high initial investments but leverage on Singapore's business-friendly environment for long-term growth

As we continue our journey through Asian franchising landscapes, Singapore stands out as a sophisticated, competitive market that can serve as both a challenging testbed and a springboard for regional expansion. It's a market that rewards quality, innovation, and strong branding, offering valuable lessons for franchise operations across Asia and beyond.

In the dynamic world of Singaporean franchising, success is not just about offering a product or service – it's about creating an experience that resonates with discerning, cosmopolitan consumers. Those who can achieve this stand to thrive not just in Singapore, but potentially across the region, leveraging Singapore's position as a global business hub and gateway to Southeast Asia.

Indonesia

Market Overview

A Tapestry of Islands and Opportunities

Indonesia has established itself as Southeast Asia's largest economy:

⇒ Population: Approximately 273 million (2021)
⇒ GDP: $1.19 trillion (2021)
⇒ GDP per capita: $4,349 (2021)
⇒ Urbanization rate: 56.6% (2021)

The franchise industry in Indonesia has seen significant growth:

⇒ Number of franchise brands: Over 700 (2021)
⇒ Number of franchise outlets: Approximately 45,000 (2021)
⇒ Franchise industry contribution to GDP: About 2% (2021)

Key sectors for franchising include:

⇒ Food and Beverage: From international fast food to local cuisine concepts
⇒ Retail: Fashion, convenience stores, and specialty goods
⇒ Services: Education, beauty, and wellness
⇒ Automotive: Car maintenance and repair services

Indonesian consumers are characterized by their youthful demographics, increasing digital adoption, and growing middle class. There's a strong appetite for both international and local brands, with an increasing emphasis on halal products and services to cater to the country's Muslim majority.

Regulatory Environment

Navigating the Regulatory Archipelago

Indonesia has a specific regulatory framework for franchising:

⇒ Government Regulation No. 42 of 2007 on Franchising: This is the primary regulation governing franchising in Indonesia.

⇒ Ministry of Trade Regulation No. 71 of 2019: This regulation provides more detailed guidelines on franchise implementation.

⇒ Registration Requirement: All franchisors must register with the Ministry of Trade before operating in Indonesia.

⇒ Local Content Requirement: At least 80% of raw materials, business equipment, and merchandise must be sourced domestically.

⇒ Disclosure Requirements: Franchisors must provide a prospectus to potential franchisees at least two weeks before signing an agreement.

⇒ Halal Certification: For food and beverage franchises, halal certification is often necessary to cater to the Muslim population.

⇒ Trademark Registration: Franchisors must register their trademarks in Indonesia before franchising.

Recent regulatory trends include increased focus on promoting local brands and protecting small and medium enterprises.

Opportunities

The Land of a Thousand Islands and Opportunities

Indonesia offers several exciting opportunities for franchising:

⇒ Large and Growing Market: With the world's fourth-largest population, Indonesia offers a vast consumer base.

⇒ Rising Middle Class: An expanding middle class with increasing disposable income creates demand for quality products and services.

⇒ Youthful Demographics: A large young population creates opportunities for youth-oriented franchise concepts.

⇒ Digital Adoption: Rapid growth in internet and smartphone usage creates opportunities for tech-integrated franchise models.

⇒ Diverse Market: Indonesia's diverse archipelago allows for regional customization and expansion strategies.

⇒ Halal Market: As the world's largest Muslim-majority country, Indonesia offers significant opportunities for halal-certified franchises.

⇒ Government Support: The Indonesian government has shown support for franchise development, particularly for local brands.

Challenges

Navigating the Indonesian Archipelago

Despite the opportunities, franchising in Indonesia comes with its unique set of challenges:

⇒ Regulatory Complexity: Frequent changes in regulations and bureaucratic processes can be challenging to navigate.

⇒ Local Content Requirements: The 80% local sourcing requirement can be difficult for some international franchises to meet.

⇒ Geographic Diversity: Indonesia's archipelagic nature presents logistical challenges for nationwide operations.

⇒ Cultural Diversity: Understanding and respecting the diverse cultural norms across different regions can be complex.

⇒ Economic Disparities: Significant income differences between urban and rural areas necessitate careful market selection.

⇒ Intellectual Property Protection: While improving, enforcement of IP rights can still be a concern in some cases.

⇒ Competition: The market is becoming increasingly competitive, particularly in urban areas and popular sectors like F&B.

Case Studies

Tales from the Archipelago

Let's examine two contrasting case studies to illustrate the realities of franchising in Indonesia:

Case Study 1: Kebab Turki Baba Rafi - Local Success Story

Kebab Turki Baba Rafi, an Indonesian kebab franchise, has become one of the country's most successful franchise stories.

Keys to success:

⇒ Affordable Pricing: Positioned as an affordable street food option, appealing to a wide demographic.

⇒ Adaptation: Successfully adapted Middle Eastern kebabs to Indonesian tastes.

⇒ Scalability: Developed a business model that could be easily replicated across the archipelago.

⇒ Halal Certification: Ensured all products are halal-certified, appealing to the Muslim market.

⇒ International Expansion: Successfully expanded to other Southeast Asian markets and beyond.

Lessons: Baba Rafi's success demonstrates the potential for local brands to achieve national and international success by adapting international concepts to local tastes and developing scalable business models.

Case Study 2: 7-Eleven - Challenges in Adaptation

7-Eleven, the global convenience store chain, faced significant challenges in the Indonesian market.

Key developments:

⇒ Market Entry: Entered Indonesia in 2009 with ambitious expansion plans.
⇒ Initial Success: Rapid expansion in Jakarta, appealing to urban consumers with its modern convenience store concept.
⇒ Challenges: Faced difficulties competing with local minimarts and traditional warungs.
⇒ Regulatory Hurdles: Struggled with regulations prohibiting convenience stores from selling alcoholic beverages.
⇒ Market Exit: Closed all outlets in Indonesia in 2017 due to franchise agreement termination.

Lessons: 7-Eleven's experience in Indonesia highlights the importance of adapting to local market conditions and regulatory environments, even for well-established global brands.

The Indonesian Way

Success in Indonesia's franchise market requires a blend of local understanding, adaptability, and patience:

⇒ Invest time in understanding Indonesia's diverse regional markets and consumer preferences
⇒ Develop strong relationships with local partners to navigate regulatory and cultural nuances
⇒ Ensure compliance with local content requirements and halal certification where necessary

⇒ Adapt products and services to local tastes while maintaining brand consistency

⇒ Leverage digital technologies to reach Indonesia's increasingly tech-savvy population

⇒ Consider a phased expansion approach, starting in major urban centres before expanding to second-tier cities and beyond

As we continue our exploration of Asian franchising landscapes, Indonesia emerges as a market of immense potential and complexity. It's a market that rewards patience, local understanding, and adaptability, offering valuable lessons for franchise operations across Southeast Asia and beyond.

In the dynamic world of Indonesian franchising, success is not just about offering a product or service – it's about becoming part of the country's diverse cultural fabric. Those who can achieve this stand to tap into one of the world's largest and fastest-growing consumer markets, with potential for expansion across the archipelago and beyond.

The Philippines

Market Overview

A Tapestry of Islands and Opportunities

The Philippines has established itself as one of Southeast Asia's fastest-growing economies:

⇒ Population: Approximately 110 million (2021)
⇒ GDP: $362.2 billion (2021)
⇒ GDP per capita: $3,298 (2021)
⇒ Urbanization rate: 47.4% (2021)

The franchise industry in the Philippines has seen robust growth:

⇒ Number of franchise brands: Over 2,000 (2021)
⇒ Number of franchise outlets: Approximately 200,000 (2021)
⇒ Franchise industry contribution to GDP: About 7.8% (2021)

Key sectors for franchising include:

⇒ Food and Beverage: From quick-service restaurants to casual dining concepts
⇒ Retail: Fashion, convenience stores, and specialty goods
⇒ Services: Education, beauty, and wellness
⇒ Healthcare: Medical and dental services

Filipino consumers are known for their brand loyalty, strong affinity for Western brands, and increasing purchasing power. There's a growing emphasis on convenience, value for money, and quality, with a particular fondness for food concepts.

Regulatory Environment

Navigating the Pearl's Regulatory Waters

The Philippines has a specific regulatory framework for franchising:

⇒ Republic Act No. 8799 (The Securities Regulation Code): Governs the registration of franchises.

⇒ Department of Trade and Industry (DTI): Oversees franchise registration and regulation.

⇒ Intellectual Property Office of the Philippines (IPOPHL): Handles trademark and patent registrations.

⇒ Philippine Franchise Association (PFA): While not a regulatory body, it promotes ethical franchising practices.

⇒ Mandatory Disclosure: Franchisors must provide a disclosure document to potential franchisees at least 10 days before signing an agreement.

⇒ Foreign Ownership Restrictions: Certain sectors have limits on foreign ownership, which can affect franchise operations.

Recent regulatory trends include increased focus on consumer protection and efforts to promote local franchise brands.

Opportunities

The Land of 7,641 Islands of Opportunity

The Philippines offers numerous opportunities for franchising:

⇒ Large and Young Population: A population of over 110 million, with a median age of 25.7 years, presents a vast market for youth-oriented concepts.

⇒ Growing Middle Class: Rising disposable incomes create opportunities for various franchise concepts.

⇒ Mall Culture: The Philippines' strong mall culture provides ample locations for franchise outlets.

⇒ OFW Remittances: Overseas Filipino Workers' remittances boost consumer spending power.

⇒ English Proficiency: High English proficiency facilitates easier communication for international franchisors.
⇒ Digital Adoption: Rapid growth in internet and smartphone usage creates opportunities for tech-integrated franchise models.
⇒ Entrepreneurial Culture: Filipinos have a strong entrepreneurial spirit, creating a large pool of potential franchisees.

Challenges

Navigating the Pearl's Complex Waters

Despite the opportunities, franchising in the Philippines comes with its own set of challenges:

⇒ Economic Disparity: Significant income differences between urban and rural areas necessitate careful market selection.
⇒ Infrastructure Issues: Logistical challenges, particularly in provincial areas, can affect franchise operations.
⇒ Intense Competition: The market, especially in urban areas, is becoming increasingly saturated in popular sectors like F&B.
⇒ Natural Disasters: The country's vulnerability to natural disasters can pose risks to business operations.
⇒ Bureaucracy: Government processes can be slow and complex, particularly for foreign businesses.
⇒ Adapting to Local Tastes: While Filipinos are receptive to foreign brands, successful adaptation to local preferences is crucial.
⇒ Intellectual Property Protection: While improving, enforcement of IP rights can still be a concern in some cases.

Case Studies

Tales from the Pearl of the Orient

Let's examine two contrasting case studies to illustrate the realities of franchising in the Philippines:

Case Study 1: Jollibee - The Filipino Fast-Food Giant

Jollibee, a homegrown fast-food chain, has become the Philippines' most successful franchise story and a formidable competitor to global giants.

Keys to success:

⇒ Local Flavour: Offered menu items tailored to Filipino tastes, such as sweet-style spaghetti and fried chicken.
⇒ Strong Branding: Developed a strong, family-friendly brand identity with its iconic bee mascot.
⇒ Aggressive Expansion: Rapidly expanded across the Philippines before going international.
⇒ Acquisition Strategy: Acquired other food brands to diversify its portfolio.
⇒ Community Engagement: Maintained strong ties with local communities through various initiatives.

Lessons: Jollibee's success demonstrates the potential for local brands to dominate the market by deeply understanding and catering to local preferences while maintaining high standards of quality and service.

Case Study 2: Subway - Challenges in Adaptation

Subway, the global sandwich chain, has faced significant challenges in the Philippine market.

Key developments:

⇒ Market Entry: Entered the Philippines in the early 2000s with its customizable sandwich concept.

⇒ Initial Growth: Expanded rapidly in urban areas, particularly in business districts.
⇒ Challenges: Struggled to compete with local fast-food chains offering rice meals, which are more aligned with Filipino dining preferences.
⇒ Market Contraction: Closed numerous outlets over the years, significantly reducing its presence in the country.
⇒ Adaptation Efforts: Attempted to introduce local flavours and rice meals to better suit Filipino tastes.

Lessons: Subway's experience in the Philippines highlights the importance of adapting to local food preferences and dining habits, even for well-established global brands.

The Filipino Way

Success in the Philippines' franchise market requires a blend of cultural understanding, adaptability, and strong operational management:

⇒ Invest in understanding Filipino consumer preferences and adapt offerings accordingly
⇒ Leverage the country's mall culture for strategic outlet placement
⇒ Develop strong relationships with local partners to navigate regulatory and cultural nuances
⇒ Embrace digital technologies to reach the country's tech-savvy population
⇒ Engage with local communities to build brand loyalty
⇒ Be prepared for intense competition, particularly in the food and beverage sector
⇒ Consider a phased expansion approach, starting in major urban centres before expanding to provincial areas

As we continue our exploration of Asian franchising landscapes, the Philippines emerges as a market of immense potential, characterized by its receptiveness to both international and local concepts. It's a market that rewards brands that can successfully blend global standards with local flavours and preferences.

In the dynamic world of Philippine franchising, success is not just about offering a product or service – it's about becoming part of the country's vibrant consumer culture. Those who can achieve this stand to tap into one of Southeast Asia's most promising markets, with potential for expansion across the archipelago and beyond.

Australia

Market Overview

A Sunburnt Country of Franchise Opportunities

Australia boasts a robust and well-established franchise sector:

⇒ Population: Approximately 25.7 million (2021)
⇒ GDP: AUD 1.98 trillion (2021)
⇒ GDP per capita: AUD 77,000 (2021)
⇒ Urbanisation rate: 86% (2021)

The franchise industry in Australia has shown steady growth:

⇒ Number of franchise systems: Over 1,200 (2021)
⇒ Number of franchise units: Approximately 80,000 (2021)
⇒ Franchise sector contribution to GDP: About 9% (2021)

Key sectors for franchising include:

⇒ Retail: Fashion, convenience stores, and specialty goods
⇒ Food and Beverage: From quick-service restaurants to gourmet coffee shops
⇒ Services: Home services, automotive, and business-to-business services
⇒ Health and Wellness: Fitness centres, pharmacies, and allied health services

Australian consumers are known for their high disposable income, preference for quality, and increasing focus on health and wellness. There's a strong appetite for both international brands and innovative local concepts.

Regulatory Environment

Navigating the Outback of Regulations

Australia has one of the most comprehensive regulatory frameworks for franchising globally:

⇒ Franchising Code of Conduct: A mandatory industry code regulated by the Australian Competition and Consumer Commission (ACCC).

⇒ Disclosure Requirements: Franchisors must provide a disclosure document to potential franchisees at least 14 days before signing an agreement or making a non-refundable payment.

⇒ Cooling-off Period: A 7-day cooling-off period after signing the agreement during which the franchisee can terminate without penalty.

⇒ Dispute Resolution: Mandatory mediation processes for franchise disputes.

⇒ Good Faith Obligation: Both franchisors and franchisees are required to act in good faith.

⇒ Unfair Contract Terms: Protection for small businesses against unfair terms in standard form contracts.

Recent regulatory trends include increased focus on fairness in franchise agreements and enhanced protections for franchisees.

Opportunities

The Great Southern Land of Franchise Potential

Australia offers several exciting opportunities for franchising:

⇒ Mature Market: A well-established franchising sector with informed consumers and experienced franchisees.

⇒ High Consumer Spending: Australians have high disposable incomes and a willingness to spend on quality products and services.

⇒ Innovation-friendly: Australian consumers are often early adopters of new concepts and technologies.

⇒ Strong Economy: A stable economy with consistent growth provides a solid foundation for business.

⇒ Multicultural Population: Diverse demographics create opportunities for a wide range of franchise concepts.
⇒ Health and Wellness Trend: Growing focus on health and wellness creates opportunities in related sectors.
⇒ Regional Expansion: Potential to use Australia as a base for expansion into the Asia-Pacific region.

Challenges

Navigating the Challenges of the Great Southern Land

Despite the opportunities, franchising in Australia comes with its unique set of challenges:

⇒ High Labour Costs: Australia has one of the highest minimum wages in the world, impacting operational costs.
⇒ Intense Competition: The mature market means high competition in many sectors.
⇒ Geographic Spread: Large distances between major population centres can create logistical challenges.
⇒ Strict Regulations: While protective, the comprehensive regulatory environment can be complex to navigate.
⇒ High Real Estate Costs: Especially in major cities, real estate costs can be a significant expense for franchise operations.
⇒ Skilled Labour Shortages: Some sectors face challenges in recruiting and retaining skilled staff.
⇒ Changing Consumer Preferences: Rapidly evolving consumer trends require constant adaptation.

Case Studies

Tales from the Sunburnt Country

Let's examine two contrasting case studies to illustrate the realities of franchising in Australia:

Case Study 1: Boost Juice - Homegrown Success Story

Boost Juice, an Australian-born juice and smoothie franchise, has become one of the country's most successful franchise stories.

Keys to success:

⇒ Health-focused Offering: Tapped into the growing health and wellness trend.
⇒ Strong Brand Identity: Developed a fun, vibrant brand that resonated with younger consumers.
⇒ Innovation: Regularly introduced new flavours and products to keep the offering fresh.
⇒ International Expansion: Successfully expanded into international markets.
⇒ Adaptability: Quickly adapted to changing consumer preferences, including introducing lower-sugar options.

Lessons: Boost Juice's success demonstrates the potential for innovative local concepts to achieve significant success in the Australian market and beyond.

Case Study 2: Starbucks - Initial Struggles and Adaptation

Starbucks, the global coffee giant, faced significant challenges when it first entered the Australian market.

Key developments:

⇒ Market Entry: Entered Australia in 2000 with ambitious expansion plans.
⇒ Initial Struggles: Faced tough competition from Australia's established café culture and preference for independent coffee shops.
⇒ Market Contraction: Closed 70% of its stores in 2008.
⇒ Adaptation and Recovery: Revised its strategy, focusing on prime locations and adapting to local coffee preferences.

⇒ Current Status: While not as dominant as in other markets, Starbucks has established a stable presence in Australia.

Lessons: Starbucks' experience in Australia highlights the importance of understanding and respecting local consumer preferences and existing market dynamics, even for well-established global brands.

The Australian Way

Success in Australia's franchise market requires a blend of innovation, quality, and cultural understanding:

⇒ Invest in understanding Australia's diverse regional markets and consumer preferences

⇒ Ensure high-quality products and services to meet Australian consumers' expectations

⇒ Develop strong systems to manage high labour costs effectively

⇒ Embrace innovation and technology to stand out in a competitive market

⇒ Ensure full compliance with Australia's comprehensive franchise regulations

⇒ Consider a phased expansion approach, starting in major urban centres before expanding to regional areas

⇒ Be prepared to adapt offerings to suit local tastes and preferences

As we continue our exploration of franchising landscapes, Australia emerges as a mature yet dynamic market. It's a market that rewards quality, innovation, and brands that can successfully blend global standards with local preferences.

In the competitive world of Australian franchising, success is not just about offering a product or service – it's about becoming part of the country's diverse and discerning consumer culture. Those who can achieve this stand to tap into one of the world's most

stable and profitable franchise markets, with potential for
expansion across the Asia-Pacific region.

New Zealand

Market Overview

A Kiwi Tapestry of Franchise Opportunities

New Zealand, despite its small population, boasts a robust franchise sector:

⇒ Population: Approximately 5.1 million (2021)
⇒ GDP: NZD 345 billion (2021)
⇒ GDP per capita: NZD 67,000 (2021)
⇒ Urbanisation rate: 86.7% (2021)

The franchise industry in New Zealand has shown steady growth:

⇒ Number of franchise systems: Over 590 (2021)
⇒ Number of franchise units: Approximately 37,000 (2021)
⇒ Franchise sector contribution to GDP: About 11% (2021)

Key sectors for franchising include:

⇒ Retail: Fashion, convenience stores, and specialty goods
⇒ Food and Beverage: Cafés, restaurants, and fast-food chains
⇒ Services: Home services, business services, and automotive
⇒ Health and Wellness: Gyms, pharmacies, and healthcare services

New Zealand consumers are known for their preference for quality, environmental consciousness, and support for local businesses. There's a growing trend towards health and wellness, sustainability, and ethical consumption.

Regulatory Environment

Navigating the Regulatory Landscape of Aotearoa

Unlike its neighbour Australia, New Zealand does not have specific franchise legislation. However, several laws and regulations impact franchising:

⇒ Fair Trading Act 1986: Prohibits misleading and deceptive conduct in trade.
⇒ Commerce Act 1986: Regulates anti-competitive behaviour.
⇒ Contract and Commercial Law Act 2017: Governs contractual relationships.
⇒ Financial Markets Conduct Act 2013: Regulates financial products and services.
⇒ Consumer Guarantees Act 1993: Provides protection for consumers.
⇒ Franchise Association of New Zealand (FANZ): While not a regulatory body, it promotes ethical franchising practices and has a Code of Practice for members.

Recent trends include increased focus on fair business practices and discussions around the potential introduction of specific franchise regulations.

Opportunities

The Land of Opportunity in the South Pacific

New Zealand offers several exciting opportunities for franchising:

⇒ High Trust Society: New Zealand's reputation for transparency and low corruption creates a favourable business environment.
⇒ Ease of Doing Business: Consistently ranked as one of the easiest countries to do business in globally.
⇒ Quality of Life: High standard of living attracts skilled workers and entrepreneurs.

⇒ Innovation-friendly: New Zealanders are often early adopters of new technologies and concepts.

⇒ Growing Tourism Sector: Pre-COVID, tourism was a significant contributor to the economy, creating opportunities for hospitality and retail franchises.

⇒ Multicultural Population: Increasingly diverse demographics create opportunities for a wide range of franchise concepts.

⇒ Gateway to the Pacific: Potential to use New Zealand as a base for expansion into other Pacific Island nations.

Challenges

Navigating the Challenges of the Land of the Long White Cloud

Despite the opportunities, franchising in New Zealand comes with its unique set of challenges:

⇒ Small Market Size: With a population of just over 5 million, market saturation can occur quickly in some sectors.

⇒ Geographic Isolation: Distance from major global markets can create logistical challenges.

⇒ High Cost of Living: Particularly in major cities, high living costs can impact consumer spending and operational expenses.

⇒ Skill Shortages: Some sectors face challenges in recruiting and retaining skilled staff.

⇒ Cultural Nuances: Understanding and respecting Māori culture and traditions is crucial for business success.

⇒ Environmental Concerns: Growing consumer focus on sustainability requires businesses to adopt eco-friendly practices.

⇒ COVID-19 Impact: While New Zealand managed the pandemic well, its tourism and hospitality sectors were significantly affected.

Case Studies

Tales from the Land of the Kiwi

Let's examine two contrasting case studies to illustrate the realities of franchising in New Zealand:

Case Study 1: Coffee Culture - Homegrown Café Success

Coffee Culture, a New Zealand-born café franchise, has become one of the country's success stories in the competitive café market.

Keys to success:

⇒ Quality Focus: Emphasized high-quality coffee and food offerings.
⇒ Community Engagement: Created welcoming spaces that became community hubs.
⇒ Local Flavour: Incorporated local ingredients and flavours into their menu.
⇒ Consistent Brand Experience: Maintained consistency across franchises while allowing for local touches.
⇒ Adaptability: Quickly adapted to changing consumer preferences, including introducing plant-based options.

Lessons: Coffee Culture's success demonstrates the potential for local concepts to thrive in New Zealand's competitive café market by focusing on quality, community, and adaptability.

Case Study 2: Esquires Coffee - From New Zealand to the World

Esquires Coffee, originally a Canadian brand, was brought to New Zealand and transformed into a global franchise success story.

Key developments:

⇒ Market Entry: Entered New Zealand in 2002, acquiring the global rights to the brand outside of Canada.
⇒ Local Adaptation: Adapted the concept to suit New Zealand's sophisticated coffee culture.
⇒ Expansion: Successfully expanded within New Zealand and then internationally.
⇒ Sustainability Focus: Emphasized fair trade and organic products, aligning with New Zealand consumers' values.
⇒ Current Status: Operates in multiple countries while maintaining a strong presence in New Zealand.

Lessons: Esquires' experience in New Zealand highlights the potential for international brands
to be successfully adapted to the local market and then used as a springboard for global expansion.

The Kiwi Way

Success in New Zealand's franchise market requires a blend of quality, innovation, and cultural sensitivity:

⇒ Invest in understanding New Zealand's unique culture, including Māori traditions and values
⇒ Focus on high-quality products and services to meet discerning Kiwi consumers' expectations
⇒ Embrace sustainability and eco-friendly practices to align with local values
⇒ Develop strong community connections and engagement strategies
⇒ Be prepared to adapt offerings to suit local tastes and preferences
⇒ Consider the potential for using New Zealand as a test market for expansion into other Pacific nations
⇒ Leverage New Zealand's reputation for quality and innovation in international expansion efforts

As we continue our exploration of franchising landscapes, New Zealand emerges as a small but sophisticated market with unique opportunities. It's a market that rewards quality, innovation, and brands that can successfully blend global standards with local values and preferences.

In the dynamic world of New Zealand franchising, success is not just about offering a product or service – it's about becoming part of the country's close-knit communities and aligning with its values of quality, sustainability, and innovation. Those who can achieve this stand to tap into a small but profitable market with potential for expansion across the Pacific and beyond.

India

Market Overview

A Tapestry of Diversity and Opportunity

India, with its vast population and growing middle class, presents a significant opportunity for franchising:

⇒ Population: Approximately 1.38 billion (2021)
⇒ GDP: USD 2.66 trillion (2021)
⇒ GDP per capita: USD 1,928 (2021)
⇒ Urbanisation rate: 34.9% (2021)

The franchise industry in India has shown robust growth:

⇒ Number of franchise brands: Over 4,600 (2021)
⇒ Number of franchised outlets: Approximately 200,000 (2021)
⇒ Franchise sector contribution to GDP: About 2% (2021), with significant growth potential

Key sectors for franchising include:

⇒ Food and Beverage: Quick-service restaurants, cafés, and local cuisine concepts
⇒ Education and Training: Tutoring centres, vocational training, and preschools
⇒ Retail: Fashion, convenience stores, and specialty goods
⇒ Services: Beauty and wellness, home services, and business services

Indian consumers are known for their value-consciousness, increasing brand awareness, and growing appetite for both international and local brands. There's a rising trend towards health and wellness, convenience, and digital services.

Regulatory Environment

Navigating the Complex Regulatory Landscape

India does not have specific franchise legislation, but several laws and regulations impact franchising:

⇒ Indian Contract Act, 1872: Governs contractual relationships, including franchise agreements.
⇒ Trademarks Act, 1999: Protects intellectual property rights.
⇒ Foreign Exchange Management Act, 1999: Regulates foreign investment in Indian businesses.
⇒ Competition Act, 2002: Prevents anti-competitive practices.
⇒ Consumer Protection Act, 2019: Provides protection for consumers.
⇒ Franchise Association of India (FAI): While not a regulatory body, it promotes ethical franchising practices.

Recent trends include increased focus on ease of doing business, digital governance initiatives, and discussions around potential franchise-specific regulations.

Opportunities

The Land of a Billion Opportunities

India offers numerous exciting opportunities for franchising:

⇒ Large and Young Population: With over 65% of the population under 35, there's a vast market for youth-oriented concepts.
⇒ Growing Middle Class: Rising disposable incomes create opportunities for various franchise concepts.

⇒ Digital India Initiative: Government push for digitisation creates opportunities for tech-integrated franchise models.

⇒ Urbanisation: Rapid urban growth opens up new markets for franchise expansion.

⇒ Diverse Market: Regional diversity allows for multiple market entries and concept adaptations.

⇒ 'Make in India' Initiative: Government support for local manufacturing can benefit certain franchise models.

⇒ Entrepreneurial Culture: Strong entrepreneurial spirit creates a large pool of potential franchisees.

Challenges

Navigating the Complexities of the Subcontinent

Despite the opportunities, franchising in India comes with its own set of challenges:

⇒ Regional Diversity: Vast cultural and linguistic differences across regions necessitate localised approaches.

⇒ Infrastructure Issues: Logistical challenges, particularly in smaller cities and rural areas, can affect franchise operations.

⇒ Real Estate Costs: High real estate prices in prime locations can impact profitability.

⇒ Regulatory Complexity: Multiple layers of regulations and frequent changes can be challenging to navigate.

⇒ Price Sensitivity: Indian consumers are generally very price-conscious, which can pressure margins.

⇒ Talent Retention: High employee turnover in certain sectors can be a challenge.

⇒ Protecting Intellectual Property: While improving, enforcement of IP rights can still be a concern in some cases.

Case Studies

Tales from the Land of Diversity

Let's examine two contrasting case studies to illustrate the realities of franchising in India:

Case Study 1: Chai Point - The Tea Revolution

Chai Point, an Indian-born tea retail chain, has successfully franchised its concept across the country.

Keys to success:

⇒ Modernising Tradition: Brought the traditional Indian chai (tea) experience into a modern retail format.
⇒ Tech Integration: Developed a strong digital presence and IoT-enabled dispensers for corporate clients.
⇒ Localisation: Offered regional tea variations to cater to diverse tastes across India.
⇒ Multiple Formats: Developed various store formats to suit different locations and customer needs.
⇒ Sustainability Focus: Emphasized eco-friendly practices, resonating with young, urban consumers.

Lessons: Chai Point's success demonstrates the potential for modernising traditional concepts and leveraging technology in the Indian market.

Case Study 2: Subway - Adapting to Local Tastes

Subway, the global sandwich chain, has had a journey of adaptation and growth in India.

Key developments:

⇒ Market Entry: Entered India in 2001 with its customizable sandwich concept.

⇒ Initial Challenges: Faced difficulties due to Indians' preference for hot, spicy foods and unfamiliarity with the sandwich concept.

⇒ Menu Adaptation: Introduced vegetarian options, local flavours (like Chicken Tikka), and spicier sauces.

⇒ Price Adaptation: Introduced lower-priced items to cater to price-sensitive Indian consumers.

⇒ Expansion Strategy: Focused on metro cities before expanding to smaller towns.

Lessons: Subway's experience in India highlights the importance of adapting to local tastes, price points, and dining habits, even for well-established global brands.

The Indian Way

Success in India's franchise market requires a blend of localisation, innovation, and strategic patience:

⇒ Invest in understanding India's diverse regional markets and consumer preferences

⇒ Develop a strong localisation strategy while maintaining brand consistency

⇒ Embrace digital technologies to reach India's tech-savvy population

⇒ Consider multiple store formats to cater to different market segments

⇒ Be prepared for intense price competition and develop strategies to maintain profitability

⇒ Invest in strong training programs to address skill gaps and reduce employee turnover

⇒ Be patient and prepared for a longer-term investment, as market penetration can take time in India

India emerges as a market of immense potential, characterised by its vast scale, diversity, and rapidly evolving consumer base. It's a market that rewards brands that can successfully blend global standards with local flavours and preferences while navigating its unique challenges.

In the dynamic world of Indian franchising, success is not just about offering a product or service – it's about becoming part of the country's rich tapestry of cultures and traditions while meeting the aspirations of its young, ambitious population. Those who can achieve this stand to tap into one of the world's largest and fastest-growing consumer markets, with potential for exponential growth and expansion.

Strategies for Successful Franchising in Asia

Adapting Your Brand

The Importance of Brand Adaptation in Asia

The importance of brand adaptation in Asia cannot be overstated. This vast continent, home to myriad cultures, languages, and consumer behaviours, presents a unique challenge to franchises seeking to expand. From the tech-savvy consumers of South Korea to the tradition-rich markets of India, successful franchises are those that can strike a delicate balance between maintaining their core brand identity and adapting to local nuances.

Key Areas of Brand Adaptation in Asian Markets

Consider the journey of Starbucks in China. When the Seattle-based coffee giant first entered the Chinese market, it faced a culture with a deeply ingrained tea-drinking tradition. Yet, today, Starbucks boasts over 5,000 stores across the country. This success didn't come from simply replicating their American model. Instead, Starbucks embarked on a journey of careful adaptation. They introduced local tea-based beverages, created larger stores with more seating to cater to the Chinese preference for leisurely coffee experiences, and even incorporated elements of Chinese culture into their store designs and product packaging. During the Mid-Autumn Festival, for instance, Starbucks offers mooncakes, a traditional Chinese delicacy, alongside their usual fare.

This level of adaptation extends to every aspect of franchising in Asia. Take the realm of product and service offerings. In the food and beverage sector, menu localisation is crucial. McDonald's, for example, offers rice burgers in several Asian countries, while KFC in China has congee on its breakfast menu. These aren't mere gimmicks, but carefully considered adaptations that resonate with local tastes and traditions.

Service customisation, too, plays a vital role. In Japan, where attention to detail and formality are highly valued, franchises must train their staff to provide a level of service that meets these exacting standards. Contrast this with the more relaxed and friendly approach preferred in Southeast Asian countries like Thailand, and it becomes clear that a one-size-fits-all approach to service is inadequate in Asia.

Marketing and communication present their own unique challenges in this diverse region. Asia's linguistic diversity necessitates careful translation and localisation that goes beyond mere word translation to conveying concepts in culturally relevant ways. Visual elements, from colours to imagery, must resonate with local aesthetics. The colour red, for instance, is considered auspicious in China but has different connotations in other Asian countries. This complexity extends to marketing channels as well. While Facebook and Instagram might be go-to platforms in many Western countries, franchises in Asia need to be adept at utilizing popular local social media platforms like WeChat in China, Line in Japan and Thailand, or KakaoTalk in South Korea.

Successful Adaptation Strategies in Asia

The 7-Eleven franchise in Japan offers a masterclass in adapting to local consumer needs. Far from being just another convenience store, 7-Eleven in Japan has become an integral part of daily life. They've expanded beyond typical convenience store offerings to include high-quality ready-to-eat meals, fresh produce, and even dry-cleaning services. They've also become pioneers in e-commerce integration and offer various services like bill payment and package delivery. This deep integration into the fabric of Japanese society has made 7-Eleven the largest convenience store chain in Japan, with over 20,000 stores.

Pricing strategies, too, must be carefully calibrated to local markets. The vast economic disparities across Asian countries mean that a pricing model that works in affluent Singapore may be entirely unsuitable for price-sensitive markets like India or Indonesia. Some franchises have found success by offering smaller, more affordable portions in these markets, allowing them to maintain their brand presence while adapting to local economic realities.

Even the physical spaces of franchise outlets require careful consideration. In the densely populated urban centres of many Asian cities, store layouts might need to be compact and efficient. Yet in countries like China, where group dining is an important social activity, larger spaces might be preferred. The aesthetics of these spaces also play a crucial role in brand adaptation. Incorporating local art or architectural styles into store decor can help a foreign brand feel more at home in its new market.

Operational processes, too, must be adapted to local norms. This extends from business practices, such as the importance of building personal relationships (guanxi) in China, to staff training programs that address local skill levels and cultural norms, including respect hierarchies in countries like Japan and Korea.

Challenges in Brand Adaptation in Asia

The path to successful brand adaptation in Asia is fraught with challenges. The sheer diversity of markets requires multiple adaptation strategies, often within a single country. Many Asian markets are evolving rapidly, necessitating constant adaptation. Franchises must also navigate the delicate balance between tradition and modernity, as many Asian consumers value both elements. The regulatory environment can be complex and varied across Asian countries, adding another layer of complexity to franchise operations. Moreover, strong local brands in many Asian markets require foreign franchises to clearly differentiate themselves.

The Future of Brand Adaptation in Asia

As we look to the future of brand adaptation in Asia, several trends emerge. With high smartphone penetration in many Asian countries, adapting to mobile-first consumers will be crucial. Environmental awareness is growing, making the incorporation of sustainable practices increasingly important. The use of AI and big data is enabling hyper-localisation, allowing franchises to create highly targeted experiences for specific Asian markets or even sub-regions. And as the line between online and offline experiences continues to blur, creating seamless O2O (Online to Offline) experiences will be key to catering to tech-savvy Asian consumers.

Conclusion

In conclusion, adapting your brand for franchising in Asia is a complex but essential process. It requires a deep understanding of diverse local markets, a willingness to be flexible, and a clear vision of your brand's core identity. Those who master this delicate balance stand to unlock significant growth opportunities in the dynamic and rapidly growing Asian franchise market. The key is to be "glocal" – globally consistent yet locally relevant. As franchises continue to navigate the rich tapestry of Asian markets, those that can tell their brand story in a voice that resonates locally while maintaining their global identity will be the ones that thrive in this exciting and challenging landscape.

Choosing the Right Franchise Model

Choosing the Right Franchise Model: Navigating the Complexities of Asian Markets

In the diverse and dynamic landscape of Asian markets, selecting the appropriate franchise model is a critical decision that can significantly impact the success and growth of a franchise operation. The right model not only aligns with the franchisor's business objectives but also resonates with the unique characteristics of each Asian market. From the bustling streets of Tokyo to the emerging economies of Southeast Asia, each region presents its own set of challenges and opportunities that must be carefully considered when choosing a franchise model.

Understanding the Asian Franchise Landscape

Before delving into specific models, it's crucial to understand the broader context of franchising in Asia. The franchise sector in Asia has experienced rapid growth over the past few decades, driven by factors such as:

⇒ Rising middle-class populations across many Asian countries
⇒ Increasing urbanisation and modernisation
⇒ Growing acceptance of Western brands and business concepts
⇒ Evolving consumer preferences and lifestyles
⇒ Technological advancements facilitating business operations

However, this growth is not uniform across the continent. Mature markets like Japan, South Korea, and Singapore have well-established franchise sectors with sophisticated consumers and regulatory frameworks. In contrast, emerging markets such as Vietnam, Indonesia, and India present vast opportunities but also come with unique challenges, including less developed infrastructure and regulatory environments.

Common Franchise Models in Asia

While there are numerous variations, the following are some of the most common franchise models used in Asian markets:

Direct Franchising

In this model, the franchisor directly grants franchise rights to individual franchisees in the target country. This model offers the franchisor greater control over brand standards and operations but requires significant resources and local market knowledge.

Example: Subway has successfully used direct franchising in many Asian countries, allowing them to maintain tight control over their brand and menu offerings while adapting to local tastes.

Master Franchising

Under this model, the franchisor grants rights to a master franchisee to sub-franchise the brand within a specific territory, usually an entire country or region. The master franchisee acts as a mini-franchisor, responsible for recruiting and supporting sub-franchisees.

Example: Domino's Pizza has effectively used master franchising in India, partnering with Jubilant FoodWorks as their master franchisee. This approach has allowed Domino's to rapidly expand across India while benefiting from local expertise.

Area Development Agreements

In this model, a franchisee is granted the right to open a specific number of units within a defined geographic area over a set period. This model is particularly useful for rapid expansion in a specific region.

Example: Starbucks has used area development agreements in China, partnering with regional operators to expand in specific provinces or cities.

Joint Venture Franchising

Here, the franchisor forms a joint venture with a local partner to develop the brand in the target market. This model combines the franchisor's brand and expertise with the local partner's market knowledge and resources.

Example: McDonald's initially entered Japan through a joint venture with Den Fujita, which helped the brand navigate the complexities of the Japanese market and consumer preferences.

Corporate-owned Stores with Eventual Franchising

Some brands choose to enter Asian markets by first establishing corporate-owned stores to build brand awareness and refine their local business model before beginning to franchise.

Example: Shake Shack used this approach when entering the South Korean market, opening corporate stores in Seoul before considering franchising opportunities.

Factors Influencing Franchise Model Selection in Asia

Choosing the right franchise model in Asia requires careful consideration of various factors:

Regulatory Environment

Asian countries have diverse legal frameworks governing franchising. For instance:

China requires franchisors to have operated at least two company-owned units for more than a year before franchising.
Indonesia mandates that franchisors prioritise local suppliers and partners.
Japan has specific disclosure requirements under the Medium and Small Retail Commerce Promotion Act.
Understanding these regulatory nuances is crucial in selecting an appropriate franchise model.

Market Maturity and Size

The size and maturity of the target market significantly influence the choice of franchise model:

In large, diverse markets like India or China, master franchising or area development agreements may be more suitable to facilitate rapid expansion.

In smaller, more mature markets like Singapore or Hong Kong, direct franchising might be more appropriate, allowing for tighter control over brand standards.

Cultural Considerations

Asian markets have distinct cultural norms that can impact business operations:

In countries like Japan and South Korea, building strong personal relationships is crucial in business dealings, which might favour models that involve closer collaboration with local partners.

In markets like China, where guanxi (personal connections) plays a significant role, joint ventures or master franchising with well-connected local partners can be advantageous.

Local Market Knowledge and Resources

The franchisor's familiarity with the target market and available resources are key considerations:

For franchisors new to Asian markets, models like master franchising or joint ventures can provide valuable local market insights and resources.

Franchisors with significant experience and resources in Asia might opt for direct franchising or corporate-owned stores for greater control.

Brand Positioning and Adaptation Requirements

The degree of localisation required for the brand can influence the franchise model:

Brands requiring significant adaptation might benefit from models like master franchising or joint ventures, leveraging local partners' expertise.

Brands with a more standardised global approach might prefer direct franchising for tighter control over brand standards.

Competition and Market Saturation

The competitive landscape in the target market is a crucial factor:

In highly competitive markets, rapid expansion through area development agreements or master franchising might be necessary to gain market share quickly.

In less saturated markets, a more measured approach through direct franchising or corporate-owned stores might be feasible.

Case Studies: Successful Franchise Model Adaptations in Asia

KFC in China: Adapting the Master Franchise Model

KFC's success in China is a prime example of effectively adapting the master franchise model. Yum! Brands, KFC's parent company, entered China through a joint venture with local partners, effectively creating a master franchise operation. This approach allowed KFC to:

- ⇒ Rapidly expand across the vast Chinese market
- ⇒ Adapt its menu to local tastes (e.g., offering congee and egg tarts)
- ⇒ Navigate complex regulatory and cultural landscapes

As a result, KFC became the largest fast-food chain in China, with over 6,000 outlets as of 2021.

7-Eleven in Japan: Area Licensee Model Success

7-Eleven's phenomenal success in Japan demonstrates the potential of the area licensee model. Seven-Eleven Japan Co., Ltd. obtained an area license for the entire country, allowing them to:

- ⇒ Tailor the convenience store concept to Japanese consumer needs
- ⇒ Develop an extensive network of stores (over 20,000 as of 2021)
- ⇒ Innovate with services like bill payment and fresh food offerings

This model enabled 7-Eleven to become deeply integrated into Japanese daily life, far surpassing its presence in its home market of the United States.

Challenges and Considerations in Franchise Model Selection

While choosing the right franchise model is crucial, it comes with its own set of challenges:

Balancing Control and Growth

Different models offer varying degrees of control and growth potential. Franchisors must carefully weigh these factors based on their strategic objectives and risk tolerance.

Adapting to Changing Market Conditions

Asian markets are dynamic, and what works today may not be suitable tomorrow. Franchisors should build flexibility into their model selection to adapt to evolving market conditions.

Managing Cultural and Operational Differences

Regardless of the model chosen, franchisors must be prepared to navigate significant cultural and operational differences across Asian markets.

Ensuring Quality Control

Maintaining consistent brand standards across different franchise models and diverse Asian markets can be challenging and requires robust systems and processes.

Future Trends in Franchise Models in Asia

As Asian markets continue to evolve, new trends in franchise models are emerging:

Hybrid Models

Increasingly, franchisors are adopting hybrid approaches, combining elements of different models to suit specific market needs. For example, a franchisor might use direct franchising in major cities while employing area development agreements for smaller markets within the same country.

Digital-First Franchising

With the rise of e-commerce and digital platforms, some brands are exploring digital-first franchise models, particularly in tech-savvy Asian markets like South Korea and China.

Social Franchising

This model, which applies franchising principles to achieve social goals, is gaining traction in developing Asian markets, particularly in sectors like healthcare and education.

Micro-Franchising

In emerging Asian economies, micro-franchising models that require lower investment are becoming popular, allowing a broader range of entrepreneurs to participate in the franchise system.

Conclusion: The Art of Choosing Wisely

Selecting the right franchise model in Asia is both an art and a science. It requires a deep understanding of the brand's strengths, the target market's characteristics, and the broader business environment. Successful franchisors in Asia are those who can adapt their models to local conditions while maintaining their core brand identity.

As Asia continues to be a key growth region for global franchising, the ability to choose and adapt the right franchise model will be a critical competitive advantage. By carefully considering the factors outlined above and staying attuned to emerging trends, franchisors can position themselves for success in the diverse and dynamic markets of Asia.

Finding and Vetting Franchisees

The Critical Importance of Franchisee Selection

In the world of franchising, the selection of franchisees is arguably the most crucial decision a franchisor will make. The right franchisees can propel a brand to new heights, while the wrong ones can lead to costly failures and irreparable damage to brand reputation. This process is not merely about finding individuals with financial capabilities; it's about identifying partners who will embody the brand's values, drive growth, and maintain consistent quality across all locations.

Understanding the Franchisee Landscape

Before delving into specific strategies, it's essential to understand the diverse landscape of potential franchisees. This pool includes established entrepreneurs looking to diversify their portfolios, corporate professionals seeking a career change, and family-owned businesses transitioning to a franchise model. Each category brings its own strengths and challenges, and successful franchisors recognize the importance of tailoring their approach to each type of candidate.

Strategies Employed by Top Franchisors

Leading franchisors employ a multifaceted approach to finding and vetting franchisees. One common strategy is participation in franchise expos and trade shows. These events provide an excellent platform for face-to-face interactions with potential franchisees, allowing franchisors to gauge initial interest and compatibility. However, savvy franchisors understand that these events are just the beginning of the process.

Another effective strategy is the development of a robust digital presence. This includes not only a well-designed website with comprehensive information about the franchise opportunity but also strategic use of social media platforms. Top franchisors create engaging content that showcases their brand culture, success stories, and the benefits of joining their network. They also utilize targeted digital advertising to reach potential franchisees based on demographics, interests, and online behaviour.

Networking within industry associations and chambers of commerce is another tactic employed by successful franchisors. These organisations often host events and provide platforms for business owners to connect, offering valuable opportunities to meet qualified candidates who are already embedded in the local business community.

The Role of Technology in Franchisee Selection

Technology has revolutionised the franchisee selection process, offering tools that enhance efficiency and effectiveness. Customer Relationship Management (CRM) systems tailored for franchise development allow franchisors to track and manage leads throughout the selection process. These systems can automate initial communications, schedule follow-ups, and provide analytics on the effectiveness of various recruitment channels.

Artificial Intelligence (AI) and machine learning algorithms are increasingly being used to analyse large datasets of franchisee performance, identifying patterns and characteristics that correlate with success. This information can then be used to create predictive models that assist in evaluating potential franchisees.

Virtual reality (VR) technology is emerging as a powerful tool in the vetting process. Some franchisors are using VR to provide immersive experiences of their business operations, allowing potential franchisees to 'visit' existing locations and experience day-to-day operations without leaving their homes. This not only saves time and resources but also helps candidates better understand the realities of running the franchise.

The Vetting Process: Beyond Financial Capability

While financial capability is undoubtedly important, top franchisors understand that it's just one piece of the puzzle. A comprehensive vetting process involves a thorough evaluation of a candidate's business acumen, operational skills, and cultural fit with the brand.

Psychometric assessments are increasingly being used to evaluate personality traits, work styles, and values. These assessments can provide valuable insights into a candidate's leadership style, ability to follow systems, and potential for success within the franchise model.

Background checks have become more sophisticated, going beyond simple criminal record searches. Franchisors are now using services that provide comprehensive reports on a candidate's financial history, legal issues, and even their online reputation.

The Importance of Cultural Alignment

Successful franchisors place significant emphasis on ensuring cultural alignment between the franchisee and the brand. This involves not just sharing similar values but also having a compatible vision for the brand's future. Many franchisors include current successful franchisees in the interview process, recognising that peer-to-peer interactions can reveal insights that might not surface in traditional interviews.

The Role of Training and Support in Franchisee Selection

Forward-thinking franchisors view the selection process as extending beyond the initial agreement signing. They recognise that comprehensive training and ongoing support are crucial for franchisee success. As such, they evaluate a candidate's willingness and ability to learn and adapt throughout the selection process. Some franchisors even incorporate trial periods or shadowing programs as part of their vetting process, allowing both parties to assess the fit before making a long-term commitment.

Leveraging Data for Continuous Improvement

Top franchisors understand that the franchisee selection process should continuously evolve based on real-world results. They meticulously track the performance of their franchisees and correlate this data with information gathered during the selection process. This allows them to refine their criteria and adjust their vetting processes over time, continuously improving the quality of their franchisee network.

The Future of Franchisee Selection

As technology continues to advance, we can expect to see even more innovative approaches to franchisee selection. Blockchain technology, for instance, could provide secure and transparent ways to verify credentials and financial information. Augmented reality might offer new ways to assess a candidate's problem-solving skills in simulated business scenarios.

However, amidst these technological advancements, successful franchisors will continue to recognise the irreplaceable value of human judgment and intuition in the selection process. The most effective approaches will likely combine cutting-edge technology with time-tested human-centric evaluation methods.

In conclusion, finding and vetting franchisees is both an art and a science. It requires a careful balance of objective assessment and intuitive judgment, leveraging both advanced technologies and traditional human-centred approaches. As the franchising landscape continues to evolve, those franchisors who can master this delicate balance will be best positioned for long-term success and sustainable growth.

Training and Support

Training and Support: The Backbone of Franchise Success in Asia

In the diverse and dynamic landscape of Asian franchising, comprehensive training and unwavering support are not merely beneficial—they are essential for success. The franchising model's strength lies in its ability to replicate a successful business across various locations. In Asia, where cultural nuances and market conditions can vary dramatically from country to country, and even city to city, the importance of robust training and support systems cannot be overstated.

Understanding the Asian Context

Before delving into specific training and support strategies, it's crucial to understand the unique Asian context. Asia is not a monolith; it's a tapestry of diverse cultures, languages, business practices, and regulatory environments. What works in Tokyo may not work in Jakarta, and strategies successful in Mumbai might fall flat in Seoul. This diversity necessitates a tailored approach to training and support that is both comprehensive and flexible.

Initial Training: Laying the Foundation

Initial training is the cornerstone of franchise success in Asia. This training must go beyond the basics of operating the business and delve into cultural sensitivity, local market dynamics, and regulatory compliance. Successful franchisors in Asia often provide:

⇒ Comprehensive Operational Training: This includes everything from day-to-day operations to quality control measures. In markets like Japan, where precision and attention to detail are highly valued, this training must be exceptionally thorough.

⇒ Cultural Adaptation Training: This is crucial in helping franchisees understand how to adapt the brand to local tastes without losing its core identity. For instance, a Western fast-food franchise might need to train its franchisees in India on how to adapt menus to suit local palates while maintaining brand standards.

⇒ Language-Specific Training: In markets where English is not widely spoken, such as China or Vietnam, providing training materials and sessions in the local language is essential for ensuring clear communication and proper implementation of franchise standards.

⇒ Regulatory Compliance Training: Given the complex and often changing regulatory environments in many Asian countries, franchisors must provide thorough training on local laws, licensing requirements, and compliance measures.

Ongoing Support: Nurturing Long-term Success

The support provided by franchisors in Asia must extend well beyond the initial training period. Successful franchisors understand that ongoing support is crucial for maintaining brand consistency and driving growth. This support often includes:

⇒ Regular Performance Reviews: Franchisors should conduct periodic assessments to ensure franchisees are meeting brand standards and financial targets. In collectivist cultures common in Asia, these reviews should be conducted with sensitivity to maintain harmonious relationships.

⇒ Continuous Learning Programmes: The fast-paced nature of Asian markets necessitates continuous learning. Franchisors should provide regular updates on market trends, new products or services, and evolving best practices.

⇒ Marketing and Promotional Support: Given the highly competitive nature of many Asian markets, franchisors must provide robust marketing support. This might include assistance with localised marketing strategies, social media management, and guidance on navigating popular platforms like WeChat in China or Line in Thailand.

⇒ Supply Chain Management: In countries with complex supply chains or import restrictions, franchisors must provide substantial support in sourcing ingredients or products. This is particularly crucial in markets like India or Indonesia, where logistics can be challenging.

Technology Integration: Bridging Distances and Enhancing Efficiency

Given the vast geographical expanse of Asia, technology plays a crucial role in delivering effective training and support. Successful franchisors are leveraging:

⇒ E-learning Platforms: These allow franchisees to access training materials and courses at their convenience, which is particularly useful in markets with significant time zone differences from the franchisor's home country.

⇒ Virtual Reality (VR) Training: Some franchisors are using VR to provide immersive training experiences, allowing franchisees to practice scenarios in a virtual environment before facing them in real life.

⇒ Mobile Apps: Custom-built apps can provide franchisees with instant access to operational manuals, training videos, and communication channels with the franchisor.

⇒ Data Analytics: Advanced analytics tools can help franchisors track franchisee performance, identify areas for improvement, and provide targeted support.

Cultural Considerations in Training and Support

When providing training and support in Asia, franchisors must be mindful of cultural factors that can significantly impact effectiveness:

⇒ Hierarchy and Respect: In many Asian cultures, there's a strong emphasis on hierarchy and respect for authority. Training programmes should be designed with this in mind, potentially involving senior management in key training sessions to underscore their importance.

⇒ Face-saving: The concept of 'saving face' is important in many Asian cultures. Support and feedback mechanisms should be designed to avoid public criticism or embarrassment.

⇒ Relationship Building: In Asia, business relationships often extend beyond the professional realm. Franchisors should consider incorporating relationship-building activities into their training and support programmes.

⇒ Indirect Communication: Many Asian cultures favour indirect communication. Training on how to interpret and respond to indirect feedback may be necessary for non-Asian franchisors.

Localisation vs. Standardisation: Striking the Right Balance

One of the biggest challenges for franchisors in Asia is striking the right balance between maintaining global brand standards and allowing for local adaptation. Training and support systems must be flexible enough to accommodate local needs while ensuring core brand values and quality standards are maintained.

Legal and Regulatory Compliance

Given the complex and often changing regulatory environments in many Asian countries, franchisors must ensure their training and support systems include robust mechanisms for keeping franchisees updated on legal and regulatory changes. This is particularly important in markets like China, where regulations can change rapidly.

Crisis Management and Business Continuity

Recent global events have highlighted the importance of crisis management and business continuity planning. Franchisors must provide training and support in these areas, helping franchisees navigate unexpected challenges, from natural disasters to public health crises.

Measuring the Effectiveness of Training and Support

To ensure the effectiveness of their training and support systems, franchisors in Asia should implement robust measurement and feedback mechanisms. This might include regular surveys, performance metrics tracking, and franchisee feedback sessions.

In conclusion, training and support are the lifelines of franchise success in Asia. By providing comprehensive, culturally sensitive, and technologically advanced training and support systems, franchisors can help their franchisees navigate the complex Asian market landscape. Those who invest heavily in these areas, continuously adapting their approaches to meet local needs while maintaining global standards, will be best positioned for long-term success in the diverse and dynamic Asian franchising market.

Quality Control Across Borders

The Paramount Importance of Quality Control in Asian Franchising

In the diverse and rapidly evolving landscape of Asian franchising, maintaining consistent quality across borders is both a critical challenge and a key determinant of success. Quality control is not merely about meeting minimum standards; it's about preserving the essence of the brand, ensuring customer satisfaction, and safeguarding the franchise's reputation across vastly different cultural and regulatory environments.

Understanding the Asian Quality Control Landscape

Before delving into specific strategies, it's crucial to appreciate the unique challenges that Asian markets present for quality control:

⇒ Cultural Diversity: Asia's cultural mosaic means that perceptions of quality can vary significantly from one market to another. What's considered high quality in Tokyo might not meet the same reception in Mumbai or Bangkok.

⇒ Regulatory Variances: Each Asian country has its own set of regulations governing quality standards, food safety, and consumer protection. Navigating this complex regulatory landscape is essential for effective quality control.

⇒ Supply Chain Complexities: The vastness of Asia, combined with varying levels of infrastructure development, can make maintaining a consistent supply chain challenging.

⇒ Skill Level Variations: The availability of skilled labour and the level of training can vary dramatically across

Asian markets, impacting the consistency of service and product quality.

Establishing Robust Quality Control Systems

To address these challenges, franchisors must implement comprehensive quality control systems tailored to the Asian context:

⇒ Standardised Operating Procedures (SOPs): Develop detailed, culturally sensitive SOPs that can be easily understood and implemented across different Asian markets. These should cover all aspects of the business, from product preparation to customer service.

⇒ Regular Audits and Inspections: Implement a system of regular, unannounced audits and inspections. In markets like Singapore or Japan, where precision is highly valued, these audits should be particularly rigorous.

⇒ Mystery Shopping Programmes: Utilise mystery shoppers who understand local cultural nuances to assess the customer experience. This can be particularly effective in markets like China or India, where customer expectations can vary significantly from Western norms.

⇒ Quality Metrics and Benchmarking: Establish clear, measurable quality metrics and benchmark performance across different markets. This allows for the identification of best practices and areas needing improvement.

Leveraging Technology for Quality Control

In the vast and diverse Asian market, technology plays a crucial role in maintaining quality control:

⇒ IoT Sensors: Implement Internet of Things (IoT) sensors to monitor critical aspects of operations, such as food temperature in restaurants or inventory levels in retail franchises.

⇒ Data Analytics: Utilise advanced analytics to identify patterns and trends in quality metrics, allowing for proactive quality management.

⇒ Mobile Inspection Apps: Develop mobile apps that allow franchisees and quality control teams to conduct and report inspections in real-time, ensuring quick identification and resolution of issues.

⇒ Blockchain for Supply Chain Transparency: Consider implementing blockchain technology to enhance supply chain transparency and traceability, which is particularly crucial in markets with complex logistics like Indonesia or Vietnam.

Cultural Adaptation in Quality Control

While maintaining consistent quality is crucial, it's equally important to adapt quality control measures to local cultural contexts:

⇒ Local Quality Perception: Understand and incorporate local perceptions of quality into control measures. For instance, in Japan, presentation and packaging are often as important as the product itself.

⇒ Communication Styles: Adapt quality feedback mechanisms to suit local communication styles. In many Asian cultures, indirect communication is preferred, and public criticism can be seen as causing loss of face.

⇒ Relationship-Based Approach: In many Asian markets, building strong relationships with franchisees can be more effective in ensuring quality compliance than purely punitive measures.

The Foundation of Quality Control

Comprehensive and ongoing training is fundamental to maintaining quality across Asian markets:

⇒ Initial Quality Training: Provide thorough initial training on quality standards, adapted to local languages and cultural contexts.

⇒ Continuous Learning: Implement continuous learning programmes to keep franchisees updated on evolving quality standards and best practices.

⇒ Train-the-Trainer Programmes: Develop local trainers who understand both the brand standards and the local culture, enabling more effective dissemination of quality control practices.

Supply Chain Management and Quality Control

Effective supply chain management is crucial for maintaining quality across Asian markets:

⇒ Supplier Vetting: Implement rigorous supplier vetting processes, considering both quality standards and local regulatory compliance.

⇒ Local Sourcing: Where possible, develop relationships with local suppliers to ensure freshness and reduce logistical complications. This is particularly important in markets like India, where there may be restrictions on imported goods.

⇒ Inventory Management Systems: Implement advanced inventory management systems to ensure product freshness and availability, which is crucial in markets with challenging logistics.

Addressing Market-Specific Challenges

Different Asian markets present unique challenges that must be addressed in quality control strategies:

⇒ China: Given the vast size of the market and varying levels of development across regions, implementing a tiered quality control system might be necessary.

⇒ India: With its diverse culinary traditions and dietary restrictions, quality control in food franchises must be particularly attuned to local preferences and regulations.

⇒ Japan: Known for its exacting standards, quality control in Japan must be exceptionally precise and consistent.

⇒ Southeast Asia: In markets like Indonesia or the Philippines, where logistics can be challenging due to geography, extra attention must be paid to supply chain quality control.

Regulatory Compliance and Quality Control

Staying abreast of and complying with local regulations is a critical aspect of quality control:

⇒ Regulatory Monitoring: Establish systems to monitor and quickly adapt to changing regulations across different Asian markets.

⇒ Compliance Training: Provide regular training to franchisees on regulatory compliance, emphasising its importance in maintaining overall quality.

⇒ Documentation and Reporting: Implement robust documentation and reporting systems to ensure regulatory compliance can be easily demonstrated when required.

Crisis Management and Quality Control

In the event of quality-related crises, having a well-prepared response is crucial:

⇒ Crisis Response Plans: Develop market-specific crisis response plans that address potential quality issues.

⇒ Communication Protocols: Establish clear communication protocols for addressing quality concerns, tailored to local media landscapes and cultural norms.

⇒ Remediation Processes: Have well-defined processes for quickly addressing and remedying quality issues when they occur.

In conclusion, maintaining quality control across borders in Asian franchising requires a multifaceted approach that combines stringent standards with cultural sensitivity and technological innovation. Franchisors who can successfully navigate the complexities of quality control in Asia's diverse markets will be well-positioned to build strong, reputable brands that resonate with local consumers while maintaining global standards. By investing in robust quality control systems, leveraging technology, and remaining adaptable to local contexts, franchisors can ensure their brand's promise is consistently delivered across the vibrant and challenging landscape of Asian markets.

Financial Considerations

Pricing Strategies

The Complexity of Franchise Pricing in Asia

In the diverse and dynamic landscape of Asian franchising, developing effective pricing strategies is a complex task that requires careful consideration of various economic, cultural, and market-specific factors. Franchisors must strike a delicate balance between ensuring profitability and remaining competitive in widely varying economic environments across the region.

20.2 Upfront Franchise Fees

Upfront franchise fees, the initial investment required to join a franchise system, can vary significantly across Asian markets and depending upon the development strategy under consideration:

⇒ Japan: Known for its mature franchise market, Japan often commands higher upfront fees. For example, a well-established international fast-food franchise might charge an initial fee of $50,000 to $100,000 USD in Japan.

⇒ China: Given the vast potential of the Chinese market, franchisors often charge substantial upfront fees, sometimes ranging from $200,000 to $500,000 USD for premium brands in tier-one cities like Shanghai or Beijing.

⇒ India: With its price-sensitive market, upfront fees in India tend to be lower. A mid-range restaurant franchise might charge between $20,000 to $50,000 USD as an initial fee.

⇒ Southeast Asia: In emerging markets like Vietnam or Indonesia, franchisors often set lower upfront fees to attract franchisees. Fees might range from $10,000 to $30,000 USD for a retail or service franchise.

Franchisors must consider factors such as brand recognition, market potential, and local economic conditions when setting these fees. Some franchisors opt for a tiered fee structure based on city tiers or market potential.

Royalties

Royalty fees, typically charged as a percentage of gross sales, also vary across Asian markets:

⇒ Japan: Given the high operational costs and mature market, royalties in Japan tend to be on the lower end, often ranging from 3% to 6% of gross sales.

⇒ China: Royalty rates in China can be higher, often between 6% to 8%, reflecting the market's growth potential and the value placed on international brands.

⇒ India: To remain competitive in the price-sensitive Indian market, royalties are often kept lower, typically ranging from 2% to 5%.

⇒ South Korea: With its tech-savvy consumers and high-value market, royalties in South Korea can range from 4% to 7%.

Some franchisors in Asia are experimenting with sliding scale royalties, where the percentage decreases as sales volume increases, incentivizing franchisees to drive growth.

Marketing Fees

Marketing fees are crucial for maintaining brand visibility and supporting franchise growth:

⇒ Singapore: In this highly competitive market, marketing fees can range from 2% to 4% of gross sales.

⇒ Malaysia: Marketing fees in Malaysia are often slightly lower, typically between 1% to 3%, reflecting the need for more localized marketing efforts.

⇒ Thailand: Marketing fees in Thailand generally fall in the 2% to 3% range, with some franchisors opting for fixed monthly contributions instead of percentage-based fees.

In markets like China and India, some franchisors are adopting a co-op advertising model, where franchisees contribute to a local advertising fund in addition to national marketing fees.

Other Fees

Franchisors in Asia often implement additional fees to cover various operational aspects:

⇒ Technology Fees: Particularly relevant in tech-savvy markets like South Korea and Japan, these fees cover the cost of proprietary software and systems. They can range from 0.5% to 1.5% of gross sales.

⇒ Training Fees: In markets with high employee turnover, like China, some franchisors charge ongoing training fees, often a fixed annual amount per outlet.

⇒ Supply Chain Fees: In markets with complex logistics, like Indonesia or the Philippines, franchisors might charge additional fees for managing the supply chain.

Market-Specific Pricing Strategies

Successful franchisors tailor their pricing strategies to specific Asian markets:

⇒ China: Given the vast disparities between tier-one and lower-tier cities, many franchisors implement a tiered pricing structure. For instance, a franchise fee in Shanghai might be double that of a tier-three city.

⇒ India: To accommodate the price-sensitive market, some franchisors offer lower upfront fees but higher royalty rates. For example, a food franchise might charge a $15,000 USD upfront fee but a 7% royalty.

⇒ Japan: With its mature market, franchisors often focus on value-added services to justify their fees. This might include sophisticated market research or cutting-edge technology support.

⇒ Southeast Asia: In emerging markets like Vietnam or Cambodia, franchisors might offer reduced fees for the first few years of operation to help franchisees establish themselves.

Currency Considerations

Given the currency fluctuations common in some Asian markets, franchisors must carefully consider how they structure their fees:

⇒ Pegged Currencies: In markets with currencies pegged to the USD, like Hong Kong, fees are often straightforwardly set in USD.

⇒ Volatile Currencies: In markets with more volatile currencies, like Indonesia or Malaysia, some franchisors opt for a local currency fee structure with periodic adjustments based on exchange rates.

Financing and Investment Considerations

Franchisors must also consider local financing landscapes when setting their fee structures:

⇒ Singapore: With its well-developed financial sector, franchisors can often charge higher upfront fees as franchisees have better access to financing.

⇒ Vietnam: In markets with less developed financing options, franchisors might offer internal financing or partner with local banks to facilitate franchisee investments.

Regulatory Impact on Pricing

Regulatory environments can significantly impact pricing strategies:

⇒ China: Recent regulations requiring franchisors to have operated at least two company-owned units for a year before franchising have led some brands to charge higher fees to recoup their initial investment faster.

⇒ Indonesia: Regulations limiting foreign ownership in certain sectors have led some franchisors to adjust their fee structures to make master franchise agreements more attractive to local partners.

Adaptation and Flexibility

Successful franchisors in Asia recognize the need for adaptability in their pricing strategies:

⇒ Performance-Based Fees: Some franchisors are experimenting with performance-based royalty structures, where fees are tied to profitability rather than gross sales.

⇒ Hybrid Models: In markets like India, some franchisors are adopting hybrid models that combine elements of franchising and licensing to create more flexible fee structures.

⇒ Long-Term Partnerships: Recognizing the importance of relationships in Asian business culture, some franchisors offer fee reductions or reinvestment programs for long-term, high-performing franchisees.

In conclusion, developing effective pricing strategies for franchising in Asia requires a nuanced understanding of each market's economic conditions, cultural factors, and regulatory environment. Successful franchisors in Asia demonstrate flexibility and creativity in their fee structures, balancing the need for profitability with the realities of local markets. By carefully tailoring their financial models to each specific Asian market, franchisors can create mutually beneficial partnerships that drive sustainable growth across this diverse and dynamic region.

Currency Risks

Understanding Currency Risks in the Asian Context

Currency risks pose a significant challenge for franchisors operating across diverse Asian markets. The volatility of exchange rates can impact various aspects of franchising operations, from initial investments to ongoing royalty payments and supply chain management. Understanding and mitigating these risks is crucial for maintaining profitability and fostering sustainable growth in the region. Franchisors must navigate a complex landscape of economic, political, and regulatory factors that influence currency movements across different Asian countries.

Types of Currency Risks in Asian Franchising

In the Asian franchising context, franchisors typically encounter three main types of currency risks. Transaction risk occurs when there's a time lag between entering into a contract and settling it, during which exchange rates may fluctuate. This can affect the value of royalty payments or supply purchases. Translation risk affects multinational franchisors when consolidating financial statements from different countries, potentially distorting the true financial picture of their Asian operations. Economic risk arises from long-term changes in exchange rates that can affect the competitiveness of a franchise in a particular market, potentially altering the fundamental economics of the franchise model in certain countries.

Market-Specific Currency Risks

Different Asian markets present unique currency risk profiles that franchisors must carefully consider. In China, the government's control over the yuan can lead to sudden policy changes affecting exchange rates. For instance, in August 2015, China devalued the yuan by nearly 2% against the USD, causing significant disruption to foreign businesses. A U.S.-based fast-food franchise might see its royalty income from Chinese operations decrease substantially in USD terms following such devaluations.

India's rupee has been historically volatile, depreciating by over 20% against the USD in 2018. This volatility, driven by the country's susceptibility to global economic events and domestic policy changes, can significantly impact franchising operations. An international coffee shop franchise might face higher costs for imported coffee beans, potentially squeezing profit margins for Indian franchisees.

Indonesia's rupiah presents another case of high volatility, particularly during economic crises. During the 1997 Asian financial crisis, the rupiah lost over 80% of its value against the USD. This level of volatility can have dramatic effects on franchising operations, with a U.S.-based retail franchise potentially seeing the USD value of its Indonesian franchise fees plummet during periods of rupiah weakness.

Strategies for Mitigating Currency Risks

Franchisors employ various strategies to mitigate currency risks in Asian markets. Natural hedging involves matching revenues and costs in the same currency where possible. For example, a U.S. pizza franchise in Thailand could source ingredients locally in Thai baht, offsetting baht-denominated revenues. Financial hedging uses instruments like forward contracts, options, or swaps to manage currency risk. A UK-based fashion franchise could use forward contracts to lock in future exchange rates for royalty payments from its Indian franchisees.

Contractual provisions offer another avenue for risk management. Franchisors might include currency adjustment clauses in franchise agreements, allowing for fee adjustments if exchange rates move beyond certain thresholds. Some franchisors opt for local currency pricing, setting fees and royalties in local currency and effectively shifting some currency risk to franchisees. This approach might require offering lower rates to compensate franchisees for the added risk. Currency diversification, achieved by operating in multiple markets, can also help spread currency risk across different economies and monetary systems.

Adaptive Pricing Strategies

To deal with currency fluctuations, franchisors often employ adaptive pricing strategies. Dynamic pricing involves adjusting prices regularly based on currency movements. A Japanese electronics franchise in Thailand might update its prices monthly based on the yen-baht exchange rate. Tiered pricing offers different pricing structures based on currency stability in different markets. A U.S. fitness franchise might offer lower royalty rates in more volatile currency markets like Indonesia, compared to more stable markets like Singapore.

Supply Chain Management

Effective supply chain management can play a crucial role in mitigating currency risks. Increasing local sourcing can reduce exposure to currency fluctuations. A global fast-food chain could switch to local beef suppliers in the Philippines to reduce USD-denominated import costs. Franchisors might also negotiate flexible supplier contracts that allow for changes based on currency movements, providing the ability to switch between suppliers in different countries as exchange rates fluctuate.

Financial Reporting and Transparency

Clear communication about currency risks is essential for maintaining strong relationships with franchisees. Franchisors should regularly update franchisees on currency risks and mitigation strategies. Scenario planning, involving the development and sharing of multiple financial projections based on potential currency movements, can help franchisees better understand and prepare for currency-related challenges.

Technology Solutions

Technology plays an increasingly important role in managing currency risks. Real-time monitoring systems enable franchisors to track exchange rate movements across multiple markets, facilitating quick decision-making. Some franchisors are also exploring automated hedging systems, using algorithmic trading to execute currency hedges more efficiently across their Asian operations.

Regulatory Considerations

Franchisors must also navigate the regulatory landscape when managing currency risks in Asia. Capital controls in countries like China can make it challenging to repatriate large amounts of profit, requiring careful financial planning and potentially local reinvestment strategies. Local currency regulations, such as Indonesia's requirement for certain transactions to be conducted in rupiah, necessitate careful structuring of franchise agreements to ensure compliance while managing currency risk.

In conclusion, currency risks present a significant challenge for franchisors operating across Asia's diverse markets. However, with careful planning, strategic use of financial instruments, and adaptive operational strategies, these risks can be effectively managed. Successful franchisors in Asia demonstrate flexibility and foresight in their approach to currency risk, enabling them to navigate the complexities of the region's monetary landscape while building sustainable and profitable franchise networks.

Repatriation of Profits

Understanding Profit Repatriation in Asian Markets

Repatriation of profits is a critical consideration for international franchisors operating in Asian markets. It involves the transfer of earnings from foreign subsidiaries or franchisees back to the franchisor's home country. This process is essential for realizing the financial benefits of international expansion, but it can be complex and challenging due to varying regulations, tax implications, and currency considerations across different Asian countries. Franchisors must navigate an intricate web of legal, financial, and operational factors to effectively repatriate profits while maintaining compliance with local laws and optimizing their tax position.

Challenges in Profit Repatriation across Asia

The challenges of profit repatriation vary significantly across Asian markets. In some countries, the process is relatively straightforward, while in others, it can be fraught with obstacles. These challenges can include restrictions on the amount of money that can be transferred out of the country, complex approval processes, high taxes on outbound transfers, and requirements for reinvestment of a portion of profits locally. Additionally, franchisors must contend with fluctuating exchange rates, which can impact the value of repatriated profits. The political and economic stability of each country also plays a role, as sudden policy changes or economic crises can affect a franchisor's ability to repatriate profits effectively.

Country-Specific Repatriation Considerations

In China, profit repatriation has become increasingly complex in recent years. The government has implemented stricter controls on outbound capital flows, requiring companies to provide extensive documentation to justify profit repatriation. Franchisors may face delays and scrutiny when attempting to transfer large sums out of the country. In contrast, Singapore offers a more favourable environment for profit repatriation, with no restrictions on the transfer of profits and a competitive tax regime that includes numerous double taxation agreements.

India presents its own set of challenges, with a complex regulatory framework governing profit repatriation. While the country has liberalized its economy significantly, franchisors still need to navigate bureaucratic processes and obtain necessary approvals from the Reserve Bank of India for certain types of transfers. In Japan, while there are no specific restrictions on profit repatriation, the country's high corporate tax rates can significantly impact the amount of profits available for repatriation.

Methods of Profit Repatriation

Franchisors employ various methods to repatriate profits from Asian markets. Dividend payments are a common approach, where the local entity distributes profits to the parent company. However, this method can be subject to withholding taxes in many Asian countries. Royalty and fee payments for services provided by the franchisor, such as marketing support or technology transfer, offer another avenue for repatriation. These payments are often subject to lower tax rates or may benefit from tax treaty provisions.

Some franchisors use inter-company loans as a means of moving money between entities, although this approach requires careful structuring to avoid running afoul of thin capitalization rules or transfer pricing regulations. Management fees for services provided by the parent company to the local entity can also serve as a repatriation mechanism, but these must be carefully documented to demonstrate their business purpose and value.

Tax Implications of Profit Repatriation

The tax implications of profit repatriation can significantly impact a franchisor's bottom line. Many Asian countries impose withholding taxes on dividends, royalties, and other payments to foreign entities. For example, China applies a 10% withholding tax on dividends paid to foreign companies, while Thailand's rate is 10% for dividends and 15% for royalties. Franchisors must also consider the tax treatment of repatriated profits in their home country, including any applicable foreign tax credits or participation exemptions.

To optimize their tax position, franchisors often leverage double taxation agreements (DTAs) between their home country and the Asian countries in which they operate. These agreements can reduce or eliminate withholding taxes and provide other tax benefits. For instance, the DTA between Singapore and Japan reduces the withholding tax on royalties from 10% to 5%, providing a significant advantage for franchisors repatriating profits through royalty payments.

Currency Considerations in Profit Repatriation

Currency fluctuations can have a substantial impact on the value of repatriated profits. Franchisors must carefully time their repatriation activities to minimize the risk of adverse exchange rate movements. Some franchisors use hedging strategies to manage this risk, such as forward contracts or options. Others maintain profits in local currencies for extended periods, waiting for favourable exchange rates before repatriation.

In countries with less stable currencies, such as Indonesia or Vietnam, franchisors may seek to convert profits to a more stable currency like the US dollar or Singapore dollar as quickly as possible to mitigate the risk of local currency depreciation. However, this approach must be balanced against any local regulations that may restrict such currency conversions.

Legal and Regulatory Compliance

Ensuring compliance with local laws and regulations is crucial when repatriating profits from Asian markets. Many countries have specific reporting requirements for outbound transfers, and failure to comply can result in penalties or restrictions on future transfers. In China, for example, companies must provide tax clearance certificates and audited financial statements before repatriating profits. In India, certain types of payments require prior approval from the Reserve Bank of India.

Franchisors must also be mindful of anti-money laundering (AML) and know-your-customer (KYC) regulations, which have become increasingly stringent across Asia. These regulations may require franchisors to provide detailed documentation on the source of funds and the purpose of transfers, adding complexity to the repatriation process.

Strategies for Effective Profit Repatriation

To navigate the complexities of profit repatriation in Asian markets, franchisors employ various strategies. Many establish regional treasury centres in countries with favourable tax and regulatory environments, such as Singapore or Hong Kong, to centralize and optimize their cash management and repatriation activities. This approach can provide greater flexibility and efficiency in moving funds between different Asian markets and back to the home country.

Some franchisors structure their Asian operations using holding companies in jurisdictions with extensive tax treaty networks, allowing them to take advantage of reduced withholding tax rates and other tax benefits. Others focus on reinvesting a portion of profits locally to support growth and demonstrate long-term commitment to the market, which can also help in obtaining approvals for profit repatriation.

Future Trends in Profit Repatriation

The landscape of profit repatriation in Asia continues to evolve. Many countries are modernizing their financial systems and regulations, potentially simplifying the repatriation process in the future. However, concerns about capital outflows and tax base erosion are leading some governments to implement stricter controls and reporting requirements. Franchisors must stay informed about these changing regulations and be prepared to adapt their strategies accordingly.

The increasing adoption of digital currencies and blockchain technology may also impact profit repatriation in the coming years. While still in its early stages, this technology has the potential to streamline cross-border transactions and reduce associated costs, although it will likely face significant regulatory scrutiny.

In conclusion, effective profit repatriation is a crucial aspect of successful franchising in Asian markets. It requires a thorough understanding of local regulations, tax implications, and currency considerations, as well as careful planning and strategic decision-making. By developing comprehensive repatriation strategies tailored to each market's unique characteristics, franchisors can maximize the financial benefits of their Asian operations while maintaining compliance with local laws and regulations.

Tax Implications

Understanding the Tax Landscape in Asian Franchising

The tax implications of franchising in Asia present a complex and diverse landscape that franchisors must carefully navigate. Each country in the region has its own unique tax system, with varying rates, regulations, and compliance requirements. Understanding these tax implications is crucial for franchisors to effectively structure their operations, maximize profitability, and ensure compliance with local laws. The tax considerations span a wide range of areas, including corporate income tax, withholding tax on royalties and fees, value-added tax (VAT) or goods and services tax (GST), and various other levies that may apply to franchise operations.

Corporate Income Tax Considerations

Corporate income tax is a primary consideration for franchisors operating in Asian markets. The rates and calculation methods vary significantly across the region. For instance, Singapore offers a competitive corporate tax rate of 17%, while Japan's effective corporate tax rate can exceed 30% when local taxes are included. In China, the standard corporate income tax rate is 25%, but certain industries or regions may qualify for preferential rates as low as 15%.

Franchisors must also be aware of the concept of permanent establishment (PE) in Asian tax laws. Establishing a PE in a country typically subjects the franchisor to local corporate income tax on profits attributable to that PE. The definition of PE can vary between countries and may be influenced by tax treaties. For example, having a representative office or providing extensive training and support to franchisees could potentially create a PE in some Asian jurisdictions, leading to unexpected tax liabilities.

Withholding Taxes on Royalties and Fees

Withholding taxes on royalties and franchise fees are a significant consideration for international franchisors. These taxes are typically levied on payments made by local franchisees to foreign franchisors. The rates can vary widely across Asia. For example, China imposes a 10% withholding tax on royalties paid to foreign entities, while Indonesia's rate is 20%. In contrast, Singapore's withholding tax on royalties is just 10%, and can be further reduced under certain tax treaties.

Franchisors often seek to mitigate the impact of withholding taxes through careful structuring of their franchise agreements and leveraging tax treaties. For instance, separating royalty payments for intellectual property from fees for specific services can sometimes result in more favourable tax treatment. Additionally, routing payments through jurisdictions with favourable tax treaties can potentially reduce the overall withholding tax burden.

Value-Added Tax and Goods and Services Tax

Many Asian countries implement a Value-Added Tax (VAT) or Goods and Services Tax (GST) system, which can have significant implications for franchise operations. These consumption taxes are typically levied on the supply of goods and services, including franchise fees and royalties. The rates and application of VAT/GST vary across the region. For example, Singapore's GST rate is 7% (set to increase to 8% in 2023), while in India, the GST system involves multiple rates ranging from 5% to 28% depending on the type of good or service.

Franchisors need to carefully consider how VAT/GST applies to their various revenue streams and factor this into their pricing strategies. In some cases, franchisors may be required to register for VAT/GST in the countries where they operate, even if they don't have a physical presence. This can create compliance obligations and potential risks if not managed properly.

Transfer Pricing Considerations

Transfer pricing is a critical issue for franchisors operating across multiple Asian jurisdictions. Tax authorities in the region are increasingly scrutinizing cross-border transactions between related parties to ensure they are conducted at arm's length. This impacts various aspects of the franchise relationship, including royalty rates, management fees, and transfer of goods between the franchisor and franchisees.

Franchisors must ensure that their pricing arrangements can be justified as being at market rates. This often requires conducting transfer pricing studies and maintaining detailed documentation to support the pricing methodology. Countries like China, India, and Japan have particularly stringent transfer pricing regulations and documentation requirements. Failure to comply with these requirements can result in significant penalties and adjustments to taxable income.

Tax Treaties and Double Taxation Avoidance

Understanding and leveraging tax treaties is crucial for franchisors operating in Asia. These bilateral agreements between countries aim to prevent double taxation and often provide for reduced withholding tax rates on cross-border payments. For example, the tax treaty between Canada and China reduces the withholding tax on royalties from 10% to 7.5% in many cases.

However, the application of tax treaties is not always straightforward. Many Asian countries have implemented anti-treaty shopping provisions to prevent the abuse of treaty benefits. Franchisors must ensure that they have sufficient substance in the jurisdictions through which they route their investments and payments to qualify for treaty benefits. Additionally, some countries, such as India, have introduced general anti-avoidance rules (GAAR) that allow tax authorities to scrutinize arrangements that they believe are designed primarily for tax avoidance.

Local Tax Incentives and Special Economic Zones

Many Asian countries offer tax incentives to attract foreign investment, which can benefit franchisors expanding into these markets. These incentives may include tax holidays, reduced tax rates, or accelerated deductions for certain types of expenditure. For instance, Thailand offers a range of tax incentives for companies investing in specific sectors or regions, including exemptions from corporate income tax for up to eight years.

Special Economic Zones (SEZs) in countries like China, India, and Vietnam often provide preferential tax treatment for businesses operating within their boundaries. Franchisors may find opportunities to establish regional headquarters or support centres in these zones to take advantage of tax benefits. However, it's important to carefully evaluate the long-term implications of relying on such incentives, as they may be subject to change or come with specific conditions that could impact the franchise business model.

Compliance and Reporting Requirements

Tax compliance and reporting requirements in Asian countries can be complex and demanding. Many jurisdictions require detailed documentation, regular filings, and in some cases, advance rulings or approvals for certain transactions. For example, China's tax system involves frequent interactions with tax authorities and requires businesses to use specific software for invoice issuance and tax filings.

The penalties for non-compliance can be severe, including financial penalties, interest charges, and in extreme cases, criminal prosecution. Franchisors must invest in robust tax compliance systems and processes, often requiring local expertise to navigate the intricacies of each country's requirements.

Emerging Tax Trends in Asian Franchising

The tax landscape in Asia is continually evolving, with several emerging trends that franchisors should monitor. Digital taxation is becoming increasingly prevalent, with countries like India and Indonesia implementing specific taxes on digital services. This could impact franchisors providing online training, support, or other digital services to their franchisees.

Environmental taxes are also gaining traction in some Asian countries, potentially affecting franchisors in sectors with significant environmental footprints. For instance, Singapore has introduced a carbon tax, which could impact franchises in the manufacturing or energy-intensive service sectors.

Another trend is the increasing focus on tax transparency and information exchange between countries. Initiatives like the OECD's Base Erosion and Profit Shifting (BEPS) project are leading to more stringent reporting requirements and greater scrutiny of international tax arrangements.

In conclusion, navigating the tax implications of franchising in Asia requires a comprehensive understanding of diverse and complex tax systems. Franchisors must carefully consider the tax impacts on their business models, structuring their operations to optimize tax efficiency while ensuring compliance with local laws. Given the constantly changing nature of tax regulations in the region, it's crucial for franchisors to stay informed of developments and seek expert local advice to manage their tax positions effectively. By doing so, they can build sustainable and profitable franchise networks across Asian markets while minimizing tax risks and maximizing after-tax returns.

Legal and Intellectual Property Protection

Trademark Registration

Trademark Registration in Asian Franchising

Trademark registration is a cornerstone of intellectual property protection for franchisors operating in Asian markets. It serves as a crucial safeguard for brand identity and reputation, which are often a franchisor's most valuable assets. The process of trademark registration in Asia, however, can be complex and varies significantly from country to country. Franchisors must navigate a diverse landscape of legal systems, cultural nuances, and bureaucratic procedures to ensure their trademarks are adequately protected across the region.

Importance of Trademark Registration in Asia

In the context of Asian franchising, trademark registration takes on paramount importance due to several factors. Firstly, many Asian countries operate on a "first-to-file" system, rather than a "first-to-use" system. This means that the first entity to file a trademark application generally has priority, regardless of who has been using the mark. This system can leave franchisors vulnerable to trademark squatting, where opportunistic individuals or companies register well-known foreign trademarks before the legitimate owner enters the market.

Secondly, the vast and rapidly growing consumer markets in many Asian countries make them attractive targets for counterfeiters and imitators. Strong trademark protection is essential for combating these threats and maintaining brand integrity. Finally, in some Asian jurisdictions, having a registered trademark is a prerequisite for taking legal action against infringers, making it a critical element of any brand protection strategy in the region.

Country-Specific Trademark Registration Considerations

China presents a unique set of challenges and opportunities for trademark registration. The country's trademark office receives millions of applications each year, making it the busiest in the world. Franchisors must be prepared for a potentially lengthy registration process, which can take up to 18 months or more. China's trademark system also requires applicants to specify the exact goods and services for which the mark will be used, using the official classification system. Franchisors should consider filing in multiple classes to ensure comprehensive protection.

In Japan, the trademark registration process is known for its rigour and attention to detail. The Japan Patent Office conducts thorough examinations of applications, including checks for similarity with existing marks. This can lead to a higher rate of initial rejections compared to some other countries, but also results in stronger protection once a mark is registered. Japanese law also recognises protection for well-known marks, even if they are not registered, which can benefit franchisors with established international reputations.

India's trademark system has undergone significant modernisation in recent years, but challenges remain. The registration process can be lengthy, often taking two to three years to complete. India also recognises "well-known" trademarks, which receive broader protection across all classes of goods and services. However, the criteria for achieving "well-known" status are stringent and typically require extensive use and recognition within India.

Regional Trademark Registration Systems

In addition to country-specific registrations, franchisors should consider regional trademark systems in Asia. The most notable is the Madrid System, which allows trademark owners to file a single application and designate protection in multiple member countries. Several Asian countries are members of the Madrid System, including China, Japan, South Korea, and Vietnam. However, notable exceptions include Thailand and Indonesia.

Another regional system to consider is the ASEAN (Association of Southeast Asian Nations) Framework on Intellectual Property Cooperation. While this does not yet provide for a unified trademark registration system, it aims to harmonise intellectual property laws and procedures among ASEAN member states, potentially simplifying the registration process for franchisors in the future.

Challenges in Asian Trademark Registration

Franchisors face several common challenges when registering trademarks in Asian markets. Language and character set differences can complicate the registration process, particularly for Western brands. In countries like China and Japan, franchisors often need to register both their original mark and a transliteration or translation in local characters. Choosing the appropriate transliteration requires careful consideration of linguistic and cultural factors to ensure the brand's essence is maintained.

Another challenge is the variation in what can be registered as a trademark across different Asian jurisdictions. For example, while many countries now allow the registration of non-traditional marks such as colours, sounds, or scents, the specific requirements and limitations vary. In Singapore, single colour marks can be registered if they have acquired distinctiveness, while in China, the registration of single colour marks is generally not permitted.

Strategies for Effective Trademark Registration in Asia

To navigate the complexities of trademark registration in Asia, franchisors should adopt a proactive and comprehensive approach. This often involves conducting thorough trademark searches in each target market before filing applications. These searches should cover not only identical marks but also similar marks that could potentially conflict.

Franchisors should also consider filing trademark applications in multiple classes to ensure broad protection. This is particularly important in countries that strictly adhere to the classification system and do not offer cross-class protection. For instance, a restaurant franchise might file in classes covering not only restaurant services but also related goods like packaged foods or beverages.

Working with local legal counsel who understand the nuances of each country's trademark system is often crucial. These experts can provide valuable insights into local practices, help navigate bureaucratic procedures, and assist in overcoming objections or oppositions to trademark applications.

Maintaining and Enforcing Trademark Rights

Registering a trademark is only the first step in protecting intellectual property rights in Asia. Franchisors must also actively maintain and enforce their trademark rights. This includes renewing registrations on time (renewal periods vary by country), using the marks consistently in commerce, and monitoring for potential infringements.

Many Asian countries require evidence of use to maintain trademark registrations. For example, in the Philippines, a Declaration of Actual Use must be filed within three years of the registration date and then again at the time of renewal. Failure to file this declaration can result in the cancellation of the registration.

Enforcement strategies may include sending cease and desist letters to infringers, working with local authorities to conduct raids on counterfeiters, and pursuing litigation when necessary. In some countries, such as China, customs recordation of trademarks can be an effective tool for preventing the import or export of counterfeit goods.

Future Trends in Asian Trademark Registration

The landscape of trademark registration in Asia continues to evolve. Many countries are modernising their intellectual property systems, introducing online filing capabilities, and working to reduce processing times. There is also a trend towards greater harmonisation of trademark laws and procedures across the region, although significant differences remain.

The rise of e-commerce and social media presents new challenges and opportunities for trademark protection in Asia. Franchisors increasingly need to consider protecting their marks not only in traditional classes but also in relation to online services and digital goods.

In conclusion, trademark registration is a critical component of intellectual property protection for franchisors operating in Asian markets. While the process can be complex and challenging, a well-executed trademark strategy can provide vital protection for a franchise brand. By understanding the nuances of each country's system, adopting a proactive approach to registration, and remaining vigilant in maintaining and enforcing their rights, franchisors can build a strong foundation for successful expansion across Asia's dynamic markets.

Franchise Agreements

Franchise Agreements in Asian Franchising

Franchise agreements form the cornerstone of the legal framework governing the franchisor-franchisee relationship in Asian markets. These contracts are essential documents that outline the rights, obligations, and expectations of both parties. In the diverse legal and business landscapes of Asia, crafting effective franchise agreements requires a nuanced understanding of local laws, cultural norms, and business practices. This section explores the key considerations, challenges, and best practices for developing and implementing franchise agreements in Asian franchising.

Key Components of Asian Franchise Agreements

While the specific contents of franchise agreements may vary depending on the jurisdiction and the nature of the franchise, several core components are typically included:

> ⇒ Grant of Franchise: This section defines the rights being granted to the franchisee, including the use of trademarks, business systems, and proprietary information.

⇒ Territory: Specifies the geographical area in which the franchisee is permitted to operate. In some Asian countries, exclusive territorial rights may be subject to specific legal requirements.

⇒ Fees and Royalties: Outlines the financial obligations of the franchisee, including initial franchise fees, ongoing royalties, and marketing contributions.

⇒ Term and Renewal: Specifies the duration of the agreement and conditions for renewal. In some Asian jurisdictions, there may be legal restrictions on minimum term lengths or renewal conditions.

⇒ Training and Support: Details the training and ongoing support provided by the franchisor. This is particularly important in Asian markets where franchisors may need to provide extensive cultural and operational adaptation support.

⇒ Quality Control and Compliance: Establishes standards and procedures to maintain brand consistency. This section often includes provisions for inspections and audits.

⇒ Intellectual Property Protection: Outlines measures to protect the franchisor's trademarks, trade secrets, and other intellectual property. This is crucial in Asian markets where IP enforcement can be challenging.

⇒ Termination and Post-Termination Obligations: Specifies grounds for termination and the obligations of both parties upon termination. This section must be carefully crafted to comply with local laws, which in some Asian countries provide significant protections to franchisees.

⇒ Dispute Resolution: Establishes procedures for resolving conflicts, often including arbitration clauses. The choice of law and forum for dispute resolution can be particularly complex in cross-border Asian franchising arrangements.

Legal and Regulatory Considerations

Franchise agreements in Asia must navigate a complex web of local laws and regulations. Some key considerations include:

⇒ Disclosure Requirements: Many Asian countries, such as China, South Korea, and Vietnam, have specific pre-contractual disclosure requirements for franchisors. These often mandate the provision of detailed information about the franchise system, financial performance, and the franchisor's business history.

⇒ Registration Requirements: Some jurisdictions, like Indonesia and Malaysia, require franchise agreements to be registered with government authorities. This process can involve scrutiny of the agreement terms and may necessitate modifications to comply with local laws.

⇒ Language Requirements: Several Asian countries mandate that franchise agreements be drafted in the local language or require local language versions to be filed with authorities. This can create challenges in ensuring consistency between different language versions.

⇒ Mandatory Provisions: Some jurisdictions specify certain provisions that must be included in franchise agreements. For example, in China, franchise agreements must include a cooling-off period during which the franchisee can unilaterally terminate the agreement.

⇒ Foreign Investment Restrictions: In some sectors, Asian countries may impose restrictions on foreign ownership or control. This can necessitate creative structuring of franchise relationships to comply with local laws while maintaining the franchisor's control over brand standards.

Cultural and Business Practice Considerations

Effective franchise agreements in Asia must also account for local cultural norms and business practices. Some important factors to consider include:

⇒ Relationship-Building: Many Asian cultures place a high value on personal relationships in business. Franchise agreements may need to incorporate more flexible terms or dispute resolution mechanisms that allow for negotiation and compromise.

⇒ Face-Saving Provisions: In some Asian cultures, the concept of "saving face" is important. Agreements might include provisions for discreet handling of compliance issues or disputes to avoid public embarrassment.

⇒ Family Business Structures: Many potential franchisees in Asia operate family businesses. Agreements may need to address issues such as succession planning or the involvement of family members in the franchise operation.

⇒ Local Business Customs: Certain business practices that are common in Western markets may be viewed differently in Asia. For example, strict non-compete clauses might be less enforceable or culturally acceptable in some Asian jurisdictions.

Adaptation and Localisation

While maintaining brand consistency is crucial, franchise agreements in Asia often require a degree of adaptation to local conditions. This might include:

⇒ Product and Service Modifications: Agreements may need to allow for local adaptations of products or services to suit market preferences or regulatory requirements.

⇒ Marketing and Advertising: Provisions related to marketing may need to account for local media landscapes and advertising regulations.

⇒ Supply Chain Management: In some Asian markets, import restrictions or local sourcing requirements may necessitate flexibility in supply chain provisions.

⇒ Training and Support: Agreements should address the need for culturally appropriate training materials and support mechanisms.

Enforcement and Dispute Resolution

Enforcing franchise agreements in Asia can present unique challenges. Key considerations include:

⇒ Choice of Law and Jurisdiction: Careful thought must be given to the governing law and forum for dispute resolution. While many franchisors prefer the laws of their home jurisdiction, this may not always be enforceable or practical in Asian markets.

⇒ Arbitration: International arbitration is often favoured in cross-border franchise agreements. However, the choice of arbitration venue and rules must be carefully considered. Some Asian jurisdictions have well-developed arbitration frameworks, such as the Singapore International Arbitration Centre or the Hong Kong International Arbitration Centre.

⇒ Injunctive Relief: Provisions for injunctive relief can be crucial for protecting intellectual property rights. However, the availability and enforcement of such relief can vary significantly across Asian jurisdictions.

⇒ Local Court Enforcement: Even with arbitration clauses, enforcement of awards may ultimately require recourse to local courts. Understanding the local judicial landscape is crucial for effective enforcement strategies.

Emerging Trends and Future Considerations

As franchising continues to evolve in Asia, several trends are shaping the development of franchise agreements:

⇒ Digital Integration: With the growth of e-commerce and digital platforms, franchise agreements increasingly need to address issues such as online sales channels, data protection, and digital marketing rights.

⇒ Sustainability and Social Responsibility: Many Asian markets are placing greater emphasis on environmental and social governance. Franchise agreements may need to incorporate provisions related to sustainability practices or community engagement.

⇒ Multi-Unit and Area Development Agreements: As franchise markets mature in Asia, there's a growing trend towards multi-unit and area development agreements. These more complex arrangements require carefully structured agreements that balance the rights and obligations of developers with the franchisor's need for control.

⇒ Cross-Border Expansion: As Asian franchisors increasingly expand across the region and globally, franchise agreements need to be flexible enough to adapt to diverse legal and cultural environments while maintaining core brand standards.

In conclusion, crafting effective franchise agreements for Asian markets requires a delicate balance between standardisation and localisation. Franchisors must navigate complex legal landscapes, cultural nuances, and evolving business practices. By working closely with local legal experts, conducting thorough due diligence, and maintaining flexibility in their approach, franchisors can develop robust agreements that provide a solid foundation for successful franchise relationships in Asia's dynamic markets. As the franchising landscape continues to evolve, regular review and adaptation of franchise agreements will be crucial to ensure they remain effective and compliant with changing legal and business environments across the region.

Dispute Resolution

Dispute resolution is a critical aspect of legal and intellectual property protection in Asian franchising. The diverse legal systems, cultural norms, and business practices across Asian countries make it essential for franchisors and franchisees to have a clear understanding of the available dispute resolution mechanisms and their implications. This section explores the various approaches to dispute resolution in Asian franchising, highlighting key considerations, challenges, and best practices.

Overview of Dispute Resolution Methods

In Asian franchising, dispute resolution typically falls into four main categories: negotiation, mediation, arbitration, and litigation. The choice of method often depends on factors such as the nature of the dispute, the relationship between the parties, local legal requirements, and the desired outcome. Each method offers distinct advantages and challenges within the Asian context, and their effectiveness can vary significantly across different jurisdictions and cultures.

Cultural Considerations

Understanding cultural nuances is crucial when approaching dispute resolution in Asian franchising. Many Asian cultures place high importance on "saving face" or maintaining dignity, which can influence the preferred methods of dispute resolution, often favouring more discreet approaches like negotiation or mediation over public litigation. There's also often a cultural emphasis on maintaining harmony and preserving long-term relationships, which can lead to a preference for collaborative dispute resolution methods that allow for compromise and mutual understanding.

Negotiation and Mediation

Negotiation and mediation are often preferred initial steps in dispute resolution due to their flexibility and potential for preserving relationships. These methods allow for creative solutions, are generally less costly than formal proceedings, and can be conducted confidentially. They often align well with Asian cultural preferences for harmony and face-saving. However, success depends heavily on the willingness of both parties to engage in good faith, and there can be challenges in enforcing outcomes, as they are typically non-binding.

To maximize the effectiveness of these methods, it's advisable to engage skilled mediators familiar with both the franchising industry and local cultural norms, ensure clear communication channels, and establish ground rules for negotiations. Many franchisors consider including mandatory negotiation or mediation clauses in franchise agreements as a first step in dispute resolution.

Arbitration

Arbitration has become increasingly popular in Asian franchising disputes, particularly for cross-border conflicts. It offers a balance between formality and flexibility and is generally faster and more confidential than litigation. Arbitral awards are often easier to enforce internationally under the New York Convention. Notable arbitration institutions in Asia include the Singapore International Arbitration Centre (SIAC), Hong Kong International Arbitration Centre (HKIAC), China International Economic and Trade Arbitration Commission (CIETAC), and Japan Commercial Arbitration Association (JCAA).

When drafting arbitration clauses, careful consideration should be given to the choice of arbitration rules and institution, seat of arbitration, language of proceedings, number and selection method of arbitrators, and scope of disputes covered by arbitration. While arbitration offers many advantages, it's not without challenges. The cost can be significant, especially for complex disputes, and some jurisdictions may have limitations on the arbitrability of certain franchise-related issues. Enforcement of arbitral awards can still be challenging in some Asian countries.

Litigation

Litigation, while often seen as a last resort, remains an important dispute resolution mechanism in Asian franchising. Court judgements carry the full weight of legal authority and can set precedents for future cases. However, litigation in Asia comes with significant challenges, including variations in legal systems and procedures across countries, potential for lengthy and costly proceedings, language barriers, and the need for local legal representation. Enforcement of foreign judgements can be problematic in some jurisdictions.

Key considerations for litigation include jurisdiction and choice of law clauses in franchise agreements, local court procedures and timelines, availability of interim relief or injunctions, and the potential for appeals. Some Asian countries, like Singapore, have established specialised commercial courts to handle complex international business disputes more efficiently, reflecting a growing trend towards transparency in judicial proceedings in many Asian jurisdictions.

Intellectual Property Disputes

Intellectual property (IP) disputes require special consideration in Asian franchising. Common IP disputes often involve trademark infringement, unauthorised use of proprietary systems, or disclosure of trade secrets. Some Asian countries have established specialised IP courts or tribunals, such as China's IP Courts and Japan's IP High Court. Many Asian countries also offer administrative enforcement options for IP rights, which can be faster and less costly than court proceedings.

However, challenges remain, including varying levels of IP protection and enforcement across Asian jurisdictions, difficulties in gathering evidence of infringement in some countries, and persistent issues with counterfeiting and trademark squatting in some markets. To mitigate these challenges, franchisors should proactively register and maintain IP rights in each operating jurisdiction, implement robust monitoring systems to detect potential infringements, and consider using a combination of administrative and judicial enforcement strategies.

Emerging Trends and Future Considerations

The growth of e-commerce and digital franchising models has led to increased interest in online dispute resolution (ODR). ODR can offer faster, more cost-effective resolution for smaller disputes or those involving parties in different locations. However, legal recognition and enforceability of ODR outcomes vary across Asian jurisdictions. Some Asian countries, like China and South Korea, have been at the forefront of integrating ODR into their legal systems.

Looking to the future, several trends are shaping dispute resolution in Asian franchising. Harmonisation efforts, such as the ASEAN Comprehensive Investment Agreement, aim to create more uniform dispute resolution frameworks across the region. There's also an increasing integration of technology, with AI and blockchain being explored for dispute resolution processes, particularly in e-commerce related franchising disputes. Many Asian jurisdictions are placing greater emphasis on alternative dispute resolution methods to reduce court backlogs and offer more flexible options. Additionally, there's growing cooperation between dispute resolution institutions across Asia to handle complex multi-jurisdictional franchise disputes.

Effective dispute resolution in Asian franchising requires a nuanced understanding of local legal systems, cultural norms, and business practices. Franchisors and franchisees must carefully consider the most appropriate dispute resolution mechanisms for their specific circumstances and jurisdictions. By incorporating well-crafted dispute resolution clauses in franchise agreements and maintaining awareness of local and regional developments, parties can establish a solid framework for addressing conflicts when they arise. As the franchising landscape in Asia continues to evolve, staying informed about emerging trends and adapting dispute resolution strategies accordingly will be crucial for successful long-term franchise relationships in the region.

Protecting Your Brand

Brand protection is a crucial aspect of franchise management, particularly in the diverse and rapidly evolving markets of Asia. A strong brand is often a franchise's most valuable asset, representing the goodwill, reputation, and customer loyalty built over time. This section explores the multifaceted approach required to effectively protect your brand in Asian franchising, covering legal, strategic, and operational considerations.

Understanding Brand Protection in Asian Markets

Brand protection in Asian markets presents unique challenges due to the region's diverse legal systems, cultural norms, and business practices. The concept of intellectual property rights varies across jurisdictions, and enforcement mechanisms can differ significantly. Moreover, the rapid growth of e-commerce and digital platforms in many Asian countries has created new vulnerabilities for brand infringement. Understanding these complexities is the first step in developing a comprehensive brand protection strategy.

Trademark Registration and Management

Trademark registration is the cornerstone of brand protection. In Asia, most countries follow a "first-to-file" system, making early registration crucial. However, the process and requirements can vary significantly between jurisdictions.

Key considerations for trademark registration in Asia include:

- ⇒ Comprehensive Coverage: Register your trademarks in all relevant classes of goods and services, including translations and transliterations in local languages.
- ⇒ Strategic Filing: Prioritize registrations based on your expansion plans and the specific risks in each market.
- ⇒ Monitoring and Renewal: Implement a system to monitor registration status and ensure timely renewals to maintain protection.
- ⇒ Local Expertise: Engage local trademark attorneys familiar with the nuances of each jurisdiction's trademark laws and procedures.

It's important to note that some Asian countries, such as China, have faced issues with trademark squatting. This practice involves third parties registering well-known foreign trademarks before the legitimate owner enters the market. To combat this, consider defensive registrations in key markets even before active expansion plans are in place.

Contractual Protection

Franchise agreements and other contractual documents play a vital role in brand protection. These agreements should clearly define the franchisee's rights and obligations regarding the use of the brand, as well as the consequences of misuse or infringement.

Key elements to include in franchise agreements for brand protection:

⇒ Detailed usage guidelines for trademarks, trade dress, and other brand elements.

⇒ Quality control measures to ensure consistent brand representation.

⇒ Confidentiality clauses to protect trade secrets and proprietary information.

⇒ Post-termination obligations, including the cessation of brand use and return of branded materials.

⇒ Dispute resolution mechanisms tailored to the specific jurisdiction.

It's advisable to have these agreements reviewed by local legal counsel to ensure enforceability under local laws and alignment with cultural norms.

Monitoring and Enforcement

Active monitoring and swift enforcement are critical components of an effective brand protection strategy. This is particularly important in Asia, where the speed of market changes and the prevalence of counterfeiting in some regions can pose significant risks.

Develop a comprehensive monitoring program that includes:

⇒ Regular market surveys and online monitoring to detect unauthorized use or counterfeit products.
⇒ Engagement with local authorities and industry associations to stay informed about potential infringement activities.
⇒ Establishment of a reporting system for franchisees and customers to alert the franchisor of potential brand misuse.

When infringement is detected, a measured and strategic approach to enforcement is crucial. This may involve:

⇒ Cease and desist letters as an initial step.
⇒ Administrative actions through local trademark offices or customs authorities.
⇒ Civil litigation in cases of significant or persistent infringement.
⇒ Criminal prosecution for counterfeiting or other serious violations, where applicable.

The choice of enforcement action should consider the severity of the infringement, local legal remedies available, and potential impact on brand reputation and business relationships.

Online Brand Protection

The digital landscape presents both opportunities and challenges for brand protection in Asia. E-commerce platforms, social media, and mobile apps have become significant channels for brand interaction and sales, but they also provide new avenues for infringement.

Key strategies for online brand protection include:

⇒ Registering domain names and social media handles proactively, including local language variations.

⇒ Implementing a robust online monitoring system to detect unauthorized use of brand elements across various digital platforms.

⇒ Engaging with major e-commerce platforms to utilize their brand protection programs and takedown procedures.

⇒ Developing a crisis management plan for addressing online brand reputation issues.

It's important to stay abreast of evolving digital trends and platform policies in each Asian market to adapt your online brand protection strategies accordingly.

Education and Training

An often-overlooked aspect of brand protection is the role of education and training. Franchisees, employees, and even customers can be valuable allies in protecting your brand if they understand its importance and how to identify potential infringements.

Develop comprehensive training programs that cover:

⇒ The value of the brand and its key elements.
⇒ Proper usage guidelines for brand materials.
⇒ How to identify and report potential infringements.
⇒ The legal and business consequences of brand misuse.

Regular refresher courses and updates on new brand protection initiatives can help maintain awareness and engagement.

Adapting to Local Markets

While maintaining brand consistency is crucial, some degree of localization may be necessary to effectively protect and promote your brand in different Asian markets. This could involve:

⇒ Adapting brand elements to resonate with local cultural preferences while maintaining core brand identity.

⇒ Developing market-specific sub-brands or product lines that align with local tastes and regulations.

⇒ Adjusting marketing strategies to comply with local advertising laws and cultural norms.

Any adaptations should be carefully managed to ensure they enhance rather than dilute the overall brand strength and protection.

Future Trends and Considerations

As Asian markets continue to evolve, brand protection strategies must adapt to new challenges and opportunities. Some emerging trends to consider include:

⇒ Increased use of AI and blockchain technologies for brand authentication and tracking.

⇒ Growing importance of sustainability and ethical branding in many Asian markets.

⇒ Potential harmonization of intellectual property laws across regional economic blocs.

⇒ Rising consumer awareness and expectations regarding brand authenticity and quality.

Staying informed about these trends and proactively adjusting your brand protection strategies will be crucial for long-term success in Asian franchising markets.

Protecting your brand in Asian franchising requires a multifaceted approach that combines legal protections, strategic planning, and operational vigilance. By understanding the unique challenges of each market, implementing comprehensive registration and monitoring systems, and fostering a culture of brand protection among franchisees and employees, franchisors can safeguard their most valuable asset and build a strong foundation for growth in the diverse and dynamic markets of Asia.

Technology and Innovation in Asian Franchising

E-commerce Integration

The integration of e-commerce into franchise operations has become a critical component of success in the rapidly evolving Asian market. This section explores the various aspects of e-commerce integration, its impact on traditional franchise models, and strategies for effective implementation across diverse Asian markets.

The Rise of E-Commerce in Asian Franchising

E-commerce has experienced explosive growth across Asia, driven by increasing internet penetration, smartphone adoption, and changing consumer behaviours. This growth has been further accelerated by the COVID-19 pandemic, which pushed many consumers towards online shopping out of necessity. For franchises operating in Asia, integrating e-commerce capabilities has shifted from being a competitive advantage to a fundamental business requirement.

The e-commerce landscape in Asia is diverse, with each country presenting unique characteristics. For instance, China's e-commerce market is dominated by giants like Alibaba and JD.com, while in Southeast Asia, platforms like Lazada and Shopee hold significant market share. In India, the e-commerce sector is seeing rapid growth with players like Flipkart and Amazon India competing fiercely. Understanding these regional nuances is crucial for franchises looking to effectively integrate e-commerce into their operations.

Challenges in E-Commerce Integration

Integrating e-commerce into franchise operations in Asia presents several challenges. One of the primary hurdles is the potential conflict between online and offline sales channels. Franchisees may perceive e-commerce as a threat to their brick-and-mortar operations, fearing cannibalization of sales. Addressing these concerns through clear communication, fair revenue-sharing models, and demonstrating the complementary nature of online and offline channels is crucial for successful integration.

Another significant challenge is the need for technological infrastructure and expertise. Many franchisees, particularly in emerging Asian markets, may lack the necessary digital skills or resources to effectively manage e-commerce operations. Franchisors must be prepared to provide comprehensive training, support, and potentially centralized e-commerce solutions to overcome these barriers.

Logistics and last-mile delivery present another set of challenges, particularly in countries with complex geographies or underdeveloped transportation infrastructure. Partnering with local logistics providers or leveraging existing franchise networks for fulfilment can help address these issues.

Strategies for Effective E-Commerce Integration

Successful e-commerce integration in Asian franchising requires a multifaceted approach. Here are key strategies to consider:

Omnichannel Approach: Implement an omnichannel strategy that seamlessly integrates online and offline channels. This could include features like click-and-collect, where customers order online and pick up from local franchise outlets or using physical stores as fulfilment centres for online orders. This approach not only enhances customer convenience but also helps alleviate franchisees' concerns about online competition.

Customized E-commerce Platforms: Develop or adapt e-commerce platforms that cater to the specific needs of your franchise system and local market conditions. This may involve creating multilingual interfaces, supporting local payment methods, and ensuring compatibility with popular local e-commerce platforms.

Data Integration and Analytics: Implement robust systems for data collection and analysis across online and offline channels. This can provide valuable insights into customer behaviour, inventory management, and sales trends, enabling franchisees to make data-driven decisions and personalize customer experiences.

Mobile-First Strategy: Given the high smartphone penetration in many Asian markets, prioritize mobile-friendly e-commerce solutions. This includes developing responsive websites and user-friendly mobile apps that cater to local preferences and usage patterns.

Training and Support for Franchisees

Comprehensive training and ongoing support are crucial for successful e-commerce integration. Franchisors should develop extensive training programs covering various aspects of e-commerce operations, including:

⇒ Digital marketing techniques
⇒ Online customer service best practices
⇒ Inventory management for e-commerce
⇒ Data analysis and interpretation
⇒ Cybersecurity and data protection

Providing continuous support through dedicated e-commerce teams, regular webinars, and updated resources can help franchisees stay abreast of rapidly evolving e-commerce trends and technologies.

Localization and Cultural Adaptation

Effective e-commerce integration in Asian franchising requires careful localization and cultural adaptation. This goes beyond mere translation of content and involves understanding local consumer behaviours, preferences, and cultural nuances. For example, social commerce is particularly popular in markets like China and Southeast Asia, where platforms like WeChat and Line play a significant role in online shopping behaviours. Adapting e-commerce strategies to leverage these local platforms can significantly enhance market penetration and customer engagement.

Payment Systems and Financial Integration

The diversity of payment preferences across Asian markets necessitates a flexible approach to payment systems integration. While credit card usage is common in developed markets like Japan and Singapore, many emerging Asian markets show a preference for digital wallets, mobile payments, or even cash on delivery. Integrating a wide range of payment options, including popular local methods like Alipay in China or GoPay in Indonesia, is crucial for maximizing conversion rates and customer satisfaction.

Regulatory Compliance and Data Protection

E-commerce operations must navigate a complex landscape of regulatory requirements across different Asian jurisdictions. This includes compliance with data protection laws, such as China's Cybersecurity Law or Singapore's Personal Data Protection Act, as well as e-commerce-specific regulations. Franchisors must stay informed about these legal requirements and provide guidance to franchisees to ensure compliance across all markets of operation.

Future Trends in E-Commerce Integration

Looking ahead, several trends are likely to shape the future of e-commerce integration in Asian franchising:

⇒ Artificial Intelligence and Machine Learning: These technologies will play an increasingly important role in personalizing customer experiences, optimizing inventory management, and enhancing predictive analytics.

⇒ Augmented and Virtual Reality: As these technologies mature, they offer exciting possibilities for enhancing online shopping experiences, particularly in sectors like fashion, home décor, and automotive franchises.

⇒ Voice Commerce: With the growing adoption of smart speakers and voice assistants, voice-enabled shopping is likely to become more prevalent, requiring franchises to optimize their e-commerce platforms for voice search and transactions.

⇒ Blockchain for Supply Chain Management: Blockchain technology has the potential to revolutionize supply chain management in e-commerce, offering enhanced transparency, traceability, and efficiency.

E-commerce integration has become an indispensable aspect of franchise operations in Asia. While it presents significant challenges, it also offers immense opportunities for growth and enhanced customer engagement. By adopting a strategic approach that combines technological innovation, cultural sensitivity, and comprehensive support for franchisees, franchise systems can successfully navigate the complex e-commerce landscape in Asia and position themselves for long-term success in this dynamic market.

Mobile Apps and Digital Marketing

The proliferation of smartphones and digital technologies across Asia has revolutionized the way franchises interact with customers and manage their operations. This section explores the crucial role of mobile apps and digital marketing in the Asian franchising landscape, examining strategies, challenges, and future trends.

The Mobile-First Asian Market

Asia leads the world in mobile adoption, with countries like China, India, and Indonesia boasting some of the highest numbers of smartphone users globally. This mobile-first environment has profoundly influenced consumer behaviour, with mobile devices becoming the primary channel for information, entertainment, and commerce. For franchises operating in Asia, developing a strong mobile presence is not just an option but a necessity for survival and growth.

The widespread adoption of mobile technology in Asia is driven by factors such as affordable smartphones, improving internet infrastructure, and a young, tech-savvy population. This digital ecosystem has given rise to "super apps" like WeChat in China and Gojek in Indonesia, which combine multiple services within a single platform. Franchises must navigate this complex landscape, deciding whether to develop standalone apps or integrate with existing platforms to reach their target audience effectively.

Developing Effective Mobile Apps for Franchises

Creating a successful mobile app for a franchise system in Asia requires careful consideration of various factors:

⇒ User Experience and Interface Design: Given the diversity of Asian markets, app design must balance global brand consistency with local cultural preferences. This may involve adapting colour schemes, icons, and navigation patterns to suit local tastes while maintaining the core brand identity.

⇒ Functionality and Features: Franchise apps should offer features that enhance customer experience and streamline operations. These may include mobile ordering and payment, loyalty programs, store locators, and personalized promotions. In more advanced markets, features like augmented reality for product visualization or voice-activated commands may be appropriate.

⇒ Integration with Franchise Operations: Mobile apps should seamlessly integrate with the franchise's backend systems, including inventory management, customer relationship management (CRM), and point-of-sale (POS) systems. This integration enables real-time updates and data synchronization across the franchise network.

⇒ Localization: Beyond language translation, effective localization involves adapting content, features, and even app functionality to suit local market needs. For example, a food franchise app in India might include a prominent vegetarian filter, while one in Japan might emphasize seasonal menu items.

Digital Marketing Strategies for Asian Franchises

Digital marketing in Asia presents unique challenges and opportunities due to the region's diverse digital ecosystems and consumer behaviours. Effective strategies often involve a mix of the following approaches:

⇒ Social Media Marketing: Platforms like Facebook and Instagram are popular across much of Asia, but local platforms such as WeChat in China, Line in Japan and Thailand, and KakaoTalk in South Korea also play crucial roles. Franchises must tailor their social media strategies to these platforms, leveraging features like WeChat's Mini Programs or Line's Official Accounts to engage customers.

⇒ Influencer Marketing: Collaborating with local influencers and key opinion leaders (KOLs) can be particularly effective in Asian markets, where consumers often place high trust in these figures. Franchises should carefully select influencers whose values align with their brand and who have genuine engagement with their target audience.

⇒ Content Marketing: Creating localized, relevant content is crucial for engaging Asian consumers. This may involve producing market-specific blog posts, videos, or infographics that address local interests and concerns. User-generated content campaigns can also be highly effective, encouraging customers to share their experiences with the franchise.

⇒ Search Engine Optimization (SEO) and Search Engine Marketing (SEM): While Google dominates in many Asian markets, franchises must also optimize for local search engines like Baidu in China or Naver in South Korea. This requires understanding local search behaviours and adapting keyword strategies accordingly.

Leveraging Data Analytics for Personalization

The wealth of data generated through mobile apps and digital marketing campaigns provides franchises with unprecedented opportunities for personalization. By analyzing customer behaviour, preferences, and purchase history, franchises can deliver tailored experiences and targeted promotions.

Implementing a robust data analytics strategy involves:

⇒ Collecting and integrating data from various touchpoints, including mobile apps, websites, social media, and in-store interactions.

⇒ Applying advanced analytics techniques, including machine learning algorithms, to derive actionable insights from this data.

⇒ Implementing personalization strategies across customer touchpoints, from customized app interfaces to targeted email campaigns and in-app notifications.

However, franchises must balance personalization efforts with privacy concerns, ensuring compliance with data protection regulations such as China's Personal Information Protection Law or Singapore's Personal Data Protection Act.

Challenges in Mobile App and Digital Marketing Implementation

Implementing effective mobile app and digital marketing strategies in Asian franchising comes with several challenges:

⇒ Technology Adoption: While many Asian markets are technologically advanced, there can be significant variations in digital literacy and technology adoption, particularly in emerging markets. Franchises may need to provide training and support to both franchisees and customers to ensure successful adoption of mobile apps and digital services.

⇒ Platform Fragmentation: The diversity of digital platforms across Asia can make it challenging to develop a cohesive strategy. Franchises may need to maintain presence across multiple platforms, each with its own technical requirements and user expectations.

⇒ Regulatory Compliance: Digital marketing and data collection practices are subject to increasing regulation across Asia. Franchises must navigate a complex landscape of privacy laws, advertising regulations, and content restrictions that can vary significantly between countries.

⇒ Cultural Sensitivity: Digital marketing campaigns that resonate in one Asian market may fall flat or even offend in another. Franchises must be acutely aware of cultural nuances and local sensitivities when developing digital content and marketing strategies.

Future Trends in Mobile Apps and Digital Marketing for Asian Franchising

Looking ahead, several trends are likely to shape the future of mobile apps and digital marketing in Asian franchising:

⇒ Artificial Intelligence and Chatbots: AI-powered chatbots and virtual assistants are becoming increasingly sophisticated, offering personalized customer service and sales support through mobile apps and messaging platforms.

⇒ Augmented Reality (AR) and Virtual Reality (VR): These technologies offer exciting possibilities for enhancing customer experiences, from virtual product try-ons to immersive brand experiences.

⇒ Voice Search and Commerce: As voice-activated devices become more prevalent, franchises will need to optimize their digital presence for voice search and explore opportunities in voice commerce.

⇒ 5G Technology: The rollout of 5G networks across Asia will enable faster, more reliable mobile experiences, opening up new possibilities for rich media content and real-time interactions.

⇒ Blockchain and Cryptocurrency: Some franchises may explore blockchain technology for loyalty programs or consider accepting cryptocurrencies as payment methods, particularly in tech-savvy Asian markets.

Mobile apps and digital marketing have become indispensable tools for franchises operating in the diverse and dynamic Asian market. Success in this arena requires a nuanced understanding of local digital ecosystems, consumer behaviours, and cultural norms. By developing robust mobile strategies, leveraging data for personalization, and staying abreast of emerging trends, franchises can create meaningful digital experiences that drive customer engagement and business growth across the region. As technology continues to evolve rapidly, franchises must remain agile, continuously adapting their digital strategies to meet the changing needs and expectations of Asian consumers.

Supply Chain Management

In the rapidly evolving landscape of Asian franchising, efficient and innovative supply chain management has become a critical factor for success. This section explores the technological advancements and strategies that are reshaping supply chain operations in the diverse and dynamic markets of Asia.

The Importance of Supply Chain Innovation in Asian Franchising

The unique characteristics of Asian markets, including vast geographical expanses, diverse regulatory environments, and rapidly changing consumer preferences, make supply chain management both challenging and crucial for franchise operations. Innovative supply chain solutions can provide a significant competitive advantage, enabling franchises to reduce costs, improve efficiency, and enhance customer satisfaction.

In recent years, the COVID-19 pandemic has further underscored the importance of resilient and adaptable supply chains. Franchises that were able to quickly pivot their supply chain strategies in response to disruptions demonstrated greater resilience and, in many cases, emerged stronger from the crisis.

Technological Advancements in Supply Chain Management

The integration of advanced technologies has been transforming supply chain management in Asian franchising. Some key technological innovations include:

⇒ Internet of Things (IoT): IoT devices are increasingly being used to track inventory, monitor transportation conditions, and optimize warehouse operations. For instance, RFID tags and sensors can provide real-time data on product location and condition, enabling more efficient inventory management and reducing losses due to spoilage or theft.

⇒ Artificial Intelligence and Machine Learning: These technologies are being applied to various aspects of supply chain management, from demand forecasting to route optimization. AI algorithms can analyze vast amounts of data to predict consumer demand patterns, helping franchises to optimize inventory levels and reduce waste. Machine learning models can also identify potential supply chain disruptions before they occur, allowing for proactive risk management.

⇒ Blockchain Technology: Blockchain is being explored for its potential to enhance transparency and traceability in supply chains. This is particularly relevant in sectors like food franchising, where consumers are increasingly demanding information about the origin and journey of their products. Blockchain can provide an immutable record of each step in the supply chain, from sourcing to delivery.

⇒ Cloud-based Supply Chain Platforms: Cloud technology is enabling better collaboration and data sharing across franchise networks. These platforms can provide real-time visibility into inventory levels, order status, and supplier performance across multiple locations, facilitating more informed decision-making and faster response to market changes.

Localization and Customization in Supply Chain Management

One of the key challenges in Asian franchising is balancing standardization with localization. While franchises strive for consistency across their operations, they must also adapt to local market conditions and preferences. This extends to supply chain management, where strategies that work in one Asian market may not be suitable for another.

Franchises are increasingly adopting flexible supply chain models that allow for localization. This might involve sourcing certain ingredients or products locally to cater to regional tastes or to comply with local regulations. For example, a fast-food franchise might source certain spices locally in India to meet consumer preferences, while maintaining a standardized supply chain for core products.

Technology plays a crucial role in enabling this flexibility. Advanced inventory management systems can handle complex product variations across different markets, while data analytics can provide insights into local demand patterns and supplier performance.

Sustainable Supply Chain Practices

Sustainability is becoming an increasingly important consideration in supply chain management, driven by both regulatory pressures and changing consumer preferences. Many Asian markets are implementing stricter environmental regulations, and consumers are showing growing interest in eco-friendly and ethically sourced products.

Franchises are responding to these trends by implementing sustainable supply chain practices. This may include:

⇒ Optimizing transportation routes to reduce carbon emissions
⇒ Implementing recycling and waste reduction programs

⇒ Sourcing from suppliers with strong environmental and ethical credentials

⇒ Using eco-friendly packaging materials

Technology is playing a key role in these efforts. For instance, AI-powered route optimization can significantly reduce transportation-related emissions, while blockchain technology can be used to verify the sustainability credentials of suppliers.

Last-Mile Delivery Innovation

The growth of e-commerce and changing consumer expectations have put increased focus on last-mile delivery in Asian franchising. Franchises are exploring innovative solutions to improve the speed, efficiency, and cost-effectiveness of delivery operations.

In dense urban areas, some franchises are experimenting with micro-fulfilment centres - small-scale distribution hubs located closer to customers. These centres, often integrated with existing franchise outlets, can significantly reduce delivery times and costs.

Technology is also enabling new delivery models. For instance, some franchises are partnering with local delivery platforms or developing their own apps to offer on-demand delivery services. In more advanced markets, there's growing interest in autonomous delivery vehicles and drones, although regulatory hurdles remain in many Asian countries.

Risk Management and Supply Chain Resilience

The COVID-19 pandemic highlighted the importance of building resilience into supply chain operations. Franchises are increasingly focusing on risk management strategies to mitigate the impact of potential disruptions.

Key strategies include:

⇒ Diversifying supplier bases to reduce dependence on single sources

⇒ Implementing advanced forecasting systems to anticipate potential disruptions
⇒ Developing contingency plans for various scenarios
⇒ Building buffer inventory for critical components or products

Technology plays a crucial role in these efforts. AI-powered risk assessment tools can analyze vast amounts of data to identify potential vulnerabilities in the supply chain. Simulation technologies can help franchises test and refine their contingency plans.

Future Trends in Supply Chain Management for Asian Franchising

Looking ahead, several trends are likely to shape the future of supply chain management in Asian franchising:

⇒ 5G Technology: The rollout of 5G networks across Asia will enable faster, more reliable data transmission, enhancing real-time tracking and communication across supply chains.

⇒ Augmented Reality: AR technology could be used to improve warehouse operations, for instance by guiding workers to the correct items or providing visual instructions for complex tasks.

⇒ Predictive Analytics: As data collection and analysis capabilities improve, franchises will be able to make increasingly accurate predictions about demand, potential disruptions, and market trends.

⇒ Circular Supply Chains: There's growing interest in circular economy principles, where products and materials are reused or recycled rather than discarded. This could lead to significant changes in how franchises manage their supply chains.

Supply chain management in Asian franchising is undergoing a profound transformation driven by technological innovation and changing market dynamics. By embracing these changes and continuously adapting their strategies, franchises can build more efficient, resilient, and sustainable supply chains, positioning themselves for success in the diverse and rapidly evolving Asian market.

Data Analytics for Franchise Performance

Data analytics has emerged as a powerful tool for optimizing performance, driving growth, and enhancing decision-making processes. This section explores the transformative impact of data analytics on franchise operations across Asia, examining key applications, challenges, and future trends.

The Rise of Data-Driven Franchising in Asia

The Asian franchising sector has witnessed a significant shift towards data-driven operations in recent years. This transition is fuelled by the increasing digitization of business processes, the proliferation of IoT devices, and the growing recognition of data as a valuable asset. Franchises across various industries, from food and beverage to retail and services, are leveraging data analytics to gain deeper insights into their operations, customer behaviour, and market trends.

The diversity of Asian markets, with their unique cultural, economic, and regulatory landscapes, makes data analytics particularly valuable for franchises operating across multiple countries. By harnessing the power of data, franchises can tailor their strategies to local market conditions while maintaining consistency in their overall brand and operational standards.

Key Applications of Data Analytics in Franchise Performance

Performance Monitoring and Benchmarking: Data analytics enables franchisors to monitor the performance of individual franchisees and compare them against benchmarks. By analyzing key performance indicators (KPIs) such as sales, customer satisfaction scores, and operational efficiency metrics, franchisors can identify top performers and those in need of additional support. This data-driven approach allows for more targeted interventions and the sharing of best practices across the franchise network.

Customer Behaviour Analysis: Understanding customer preferences and behaviour patterns is crucial for franchise success. Advanced analytics techniques, including predictive modelling and sentiment analysis, allow franchises to gain deeper insights into customer needs and expectations. This information can be used to personalize marketing efforts, optimize product offerings, and enhance the overall customer experience.

Inventory and Supply Chain Optimization: Data analytics plays a crucial role in optimizing inventory management and supply chain operations. By analyzing historical sales data, seasonal trends, and external factors such as local events or weather patterns, franchises can more accurately forecast demand and adjust inventory levels accordingly. This helps reduce waste, minimize stockouts, and improve overall supply chain efficiency.

Location Intelligence: For franchises looking to expand, data analytics can provide valuable insights into optimal locations for new outlets. By analyzing demographic data, foot traffic patterns, competitor locations, and other relevant factors, franchises can make more informed decisions about where to open new stores, reducing the risk of poor location choices.

Marketing ROI and Campaign Optimization: Data analytics enables franchises to measure the effectiveness of their marketing campaigns more accurately. By tracking customer engagement across various channels and correlating it with sales data, franchises can determine which marketing strategies are most effective in different markets. This allows for more efficient allocation of marketing budgets and the development of targeted, data-driven marketing campaigns.

Challenges in Implementing Data Analytics in Asian Franchising

While the benefits of data analytics are clear, implementing effective data analytics strategies in Asian franchising comes with several challenges:

⇒ Data Quality and Integration: Many franchises struggle with data quality issues, particularly when dealing with data from multiple sources and across different countries. Integrating data from various systems and ensuring its accuracy and consistency can be a significant challenge.

⇒ Data Privacy and Regulatory Compliance: Asian countries have diverse data protection laws, and navigating this complex regulatory landscape can be challenging for franchises operating across multiple markets. Ensuring compliance with local regulations while still leveraging data for business insights requires careful planning and robust data governance practices.

⇒ Cultural Differences in Data Sharing: In some Asian cultures, there may be resistance to sharing data, particularly financial or operational data, which can hinder the implementation of comprehensive data analytics strategies across the franchise network.

⇒ Technological Infrastructure: The level of technological infrastructure varies significantly across Asian countries. Franchises operating in less developed markets may face challenges in implementing advanced data analytics solutions due to limited internet connectivity or lack of access to sophisticated hardware and software.

⇒ Skills Gap: There is often a shortage of skilled data analysts and data scientists in many Asian markets. Franchises may struggle to find and retain talent capable of implementing and managing advanced analytics initiatives.

Best Practices for Implementing Data Analytics in Asian Franchising

To overcome these challenges and maximize the benefits of data analytics, franchises operating in Asia should consider the following best practices:

⇒ Develop a Clear Data Strategy: Start by defining clear objectives for your data analytics initiatives. Identify the key questions you want to answer and the specific business outcomes you hope to achieve through data-driven insights.

⇒ Invest in Data Infrastructure: Implement robust data collection and storage systems that can handle large volumes of data from diverse sources. Consider cloud-based solutions that can scale with your franchise's growth and provide flexibility in data management.

⇒ Ensure Data Quality: Implement data governance practices to ensure the accuracy, consistency, and reliability of your data. This may include data cleansing processes, standardized data entry procedures, and regular data quality audits.

⇒ Prioritize Data Security and Privacy: Develop comprehensive data security and privacy policies that comply with local regulations across all markets where you operate. Implement strong security measures to protect sensitive data and build trust with franchisees and customers.

⇒ Foster a Data-Driven Culture: Encourage a culture of data-driven decision-making across your franchise network. Provide training and support to help franchisees understand the value of data analytics and how to use insights effectively in their operations.

⇒ Start Small and Scale: Begin with pilot projects focused on specific, high-impact areas before rolling out comprehensive data analytics initiatives. This approach allows you to demonstrate value quickly and refine your strategies based on early learnings.

Emerging Trends in Data Analytics for Asian Franchising

⇒ As technology continues to evolve, several emerging trends are shaping the future of data analytics in Asian franchising:

⇒ Artificial Intelligence and Machine Learning: AI and ML algorithms are becoming increasingly sophisticated, enabling more accurate predictive analytics and automated decision-making processes.

⇒ Real-Time Analytics: With the growth of IoT devices and 5G networks, franchises are moving towards real-time data analytics, allowing for more agile responses to changing market conditions.

⇒ Edge Computing: This technology allows data processing to occur closer to the source of data generation, reducing latency and enabling faster insights, particularly useful for franchises with geographically dispersed operations.

⇒ Natural Language Processing: NLP technologies are making it easier to analyze unstructured data sources such as customer reviews, social media posts, and support tickets, providing richer insights into customer sentiment and preferences.

⇒ Augmented Analytics: This emerging field combines AI and natural language generation to automate data preparation and insight discovery, making advanced analytics more accessible to non-technical users within the franchise network.

By leveraging data-driven insights, franchises can enhance their decision-making processes, optimize operations, and deliver better experiences to their customers. While challenges exist, particularly in terms of data integration, privacy, and cultural adaptation, the potential benefits of data analytics far outweigh the obstacles. As technology continues to advance, franchises that successfully harness the power of data analytics will be well-positioned to thrive in the competitive Asian franchising landscape.

Navigating Cultural Differences

Communication Styles

Effective communication is the bedrock of successful franchise operations, particularly in the diverse cultural landscape of Asia. Understanding and adapting to various communication styles across different Asian cultures is crucial for franchisors and franchisees alike. This section delves into the nuances of communication styles prevalent in Asian business contexts, offering insights and strategies for navigating these differences.

High-Context vs. Low-Context Communication

One of the fundamental distinctions in communication styles across cultures is the concept of high-context versus low-context communication, as proposed by anthropologist Edward T. Hall. This framework is particularly relevant when examining communication patterns in Asian cultures.

High-context communication, prevalent in many Asian cultures such as China, Japan, and Korea, relies heavily on implicit understanding and non-verbal cues. In these cultures, much of the message is conveyed through context, tone, body language, and shared cultural knowledge. The spoken word is often less direct, with an emphasis on maintaining harmony and avoiding confrontation. For example, in a Japanese business setting, a polite "we will consider it" might actually mean "no," but is expressed indirectly to preserve face and avoid outright rejection.

Low-context communication, more common in Western cultures, tends to be more explicit and direct. The message is primarily conveyed through clear, specific language with less reliance on context or non-verbal cues. While some Asian cultures, such as Singapore, have adopted more direct communication styles due to Western influences, many still lean towards high-context communication.

For franchises operating across these different communication contexts, awareness and adaptation are key. A franchisor from a low-context culture might need to learn to read between the lines when communicating with franchisees in high-context cultures. Conversely, franchisees from high-context cultures may need to adjust to more direct communication styles when dealing with Western franchisors or customers.

Hierarchical vs. Egalitarian Communication

Another significant aspect of communication in Asian business contexts is the influence of hierarchy. Many Asian cultures, influenced by Confucian values, place great importance on hierarchical relationships and respect for authority.

In hierarchical communication systems, common in countries like China, Japan, and Korea, communication often flows from top to bottom. Junior employees or franchisees may be hesitant to voice opinions or disagree with superiors openly. Decision-making typically occurs at higher levels of the organization, with expectations that these decisions will be implemented without question.

This hierarchical approach can present challenges for franchises accustomed to more egalitarian communication styles. For instance, a Western franchisor might expect open feedback and suggestions from franchisees but may find Asian franchisees reluctant to offer critiques or alternative ideas, especially in group settings.

To navigate these differences, franchisors might consider implementing communication channels that allow for more indirect feedback, such as anonymous suggestion systems or one-on-one meetings. It's also crucial to be mindful of age and seniority when communicating, as these factors often play a significant role in hierarchical cultures.

Relationship-Oriented vs. Task-Oriented Communication

The emphasis on relationship-building in business communications varies significantly across cultures. Many Asian cultures prioritize establishing and maintaining relationships (guanxi in Chinese business culture) as a foundation for business interactions.

In relationship-oriented communication styles, common in countries like China, Vietnam, and Indonesia, significant time and effort are invested in building personal connections before delving into business matters. Small talk, sharing meals, and socializing outside of work are considered essential components of business communication.

In contrast, task-oriented communication styles, more prevalent in Western business cultures and some Asian countries like Singapore, focus more directly on the business at hand. Efficiency and getting to the point are valued, with less emphasis on personal relationship-building.

For franchises navigating these different approaches, it's important to allocate time for relationship-building activities, especially in the initial stages of partnerships in relationship-oriented cultures. This might involve extended visits, participation in social activities, and patience in allowing business relationships to develop organically.

Non-Verbal Communication and Saving Face

Non-verbal communication plays a crucial role in many Asian cultures, particularly in high-context communication systems. Gestures, facial expressions, and body language can often convey as much, if not more, than spoken words.

The concept of "saving face" is paramount in many Asian cultures. This involves maintaining one's dignity and the dignity of others in social interactions. Communication styles in these cultures often aim to avoid causing embarrassment or loss of face for any party involved.

For example, in many Asian cultures, saying "no" directly is considered impolite and may cause loss of face. Instead, indirect refusals or non-committal responses are often used. Similarly, public criticism or disagreement, especially with superiors, is generally avoided to preserve harmony and face.

Franchisors and franchisees operating in Asian markets need to be attuned to these non-verbal cues and the importance of face-saving behaviours. This might involve learning to communicate disagreement or negative feedback in more indirect ways, being cautious about putting someone on the spot in public settings and paying attention to subtle changes in body language or tone that might indicate discomfort or disagreement.

Language and Translation Challenges

While English is widely used in international business, including in many Asian countries, language differences can still pose significant challenges in franchise communications. Even when a common language is spoken, nuances, idioms, and cultural references can lead to misunderstandings.

The use of translators or interpreters is common in many Asian business settings, particularly for complex negotiations or legal discussions. However, it's important to recognize that translation is not just about converting words from one language to another, but also about conveying cultural context and meaning.

Franchises operating across linguistic boundaries should consider investing in professional translation services, particularly for key documents such as franchise agreements, operations manuals, and marketing materials. It's also beneficial to have bilingual staff members who understand both the language and the cultural nuances of communication.

Adapting Communication Styles in a Franchise Context

Given the diversity of communication styles across Asian cultures, franchises must develop strategies to adapt and bridge these differences effectively. Some key approaches include:

⇒ Cultural Training: Provide comprehensive cultural training for both franchisors and franchisees, focusing on communication styles, business etiquette, and cultural sensitivities specific to each market.

⇒ Flexible Communication Channels: Implement a variety of communication channels to accommodate different preferences. For example, some cultures may prefer face-to-face meetings, while others might be more comfortable with written communication or technology-mediated interactions.

⇒ Clear Guidelines: Develop clear communication guidelines within the franchise system that acknowledge and respect cultural differences while establishing a common framework for interaction.

⇒ Local Adaptation: Encourage local adaptation of communication strategies. What works in one Asian market may not be effective in another, so flexibility and local insight are crucial.

⇒ Building Cultural Intelligence: Foster cultural intelligence within the organization, encouraging curiosity, openness, and adaptability in cross-cultural communications.

By recognizing the nuances of high-context vs. low-context communication, hierarchical influences, relationship-oriented approaches, non-verbal cues, and language challenges, franchises can develop more effective communication strategies. This cultural sensitivity not only helps in avoiding misunderstandings but also in building stronger, more productive relationships across the franchise network. As Asian markets continue to evolve and globalize, the ability to bridge these communication differences will remain a key competency for successful franchise operations in the region.

Business Etiquette

This section explores the nuances of business etiquette across various Asian cultures, highlighting key areas where franchisors and franchisees must pay particular attention to cultural norms and expectations.

The Importance of Business Etiquette in Asian Franchising

Business etiquette in Asia goes far beyond simple politeness; it is an essential component of professional interactions that can significantly impact the success of franchise operations. In many Asian cultures, the way one conducts oneself in business settings is seen as a reflection of one's character, professionalism, and respect for local customs. Missteps in etiquette can lead to misunderstandings, loss of face, and even the breakdown of business relationships.

For franchises operating across multiple Asian markets, navigating the diverse landscape of business etiquette can be challenging. What is considered appropriate in one country may be viewed as offensive in another. Therefore, a nuanced understanding of local customs and practices is essential for franchisors and franchisees alike.

Greetings and Introductions

The manner of greeting and introducing oneself varies significantly across Asian cultures and can set the tone for the entire business interaction.

In Japan, for instance, the bow is the traditional form of greeting. The depth and duration of the bow can convey respect, apology, or gratitude, depending on the context. While handshakes are becoming more common in international business settings, it's important to wait for the Japanese counterpart to initiate a handshake.

In contrast, in countries like India and Thailand, the traditional greeting involves pressing the palms together in a prayer-like gesture. This is accompanied by saying "Namaste" in India or "Wai" in Thailand. The height at which the hands are held can indicate the level of respect being shown.

In China and Korea, a slight nod or bow is common, often accompanied by a handshake. It's important to note that in many Asian cultures, including China, Korea, and Japan, it's customary to greet the most senior person first.

When it comes to introductions, the use of titles and formal names is crucial in many Asian business contexts. In Japan and Korea, for example, it's respectful to use a person's last name followed by their title (e.g., "Kim-sajangnim" in Korean, where "sajangnim" means "president"). In China, the family name comes first, followed by the given name.

Franchisors and franchisees should take care to learn and use the appropriate forms of address for each culture they operate in. It's also advisable to have business cards prepared in both English and the local language, and to present and receive them with both hands as a sign of respect in many Asian cultures.

Gift-Giving Customs

Gift-giving is an important aspect of business etiquette in many Asian cultures, often used to build relationships and show appreciation. However, the customs surrounding gift-giving vary significantly across the region.

In Japan, gift-giving is a highly ritualized practice. Gifts should be beautifully wrapped and presented with both hands. It's customary to exchange gifts at the end of a meeting or business dinner. The recipient will often decline the gift once or twice before accepting, as a show of modesty.

In China, gifts are also common in business settings, but there are some important considerations. Clocks are considered unlucky gifts as they are associated with death. The number four is also considered unlucky, so gifts should not be given in sets of four. On the other hand, the number eight is considered lucky.

In some countries, such as Singapore and Malaysia, gift-giving in business settings is less common and may even be viewed with suspicion, particularly when dealing with government officials. It's important to be aware of local anti-corruption laws and company policies regarding gift-giving.

For franchises operating across multiple Asian markets, it's advisable to develop clear guidelines on gift-giving that take into account local customs and legal considerations. When in doubt, small gifts that represent one's home country or company are often appreciated.

Business Meetings and Negotiations

The conduct of business meetings and negotiations varies significantly across Asian cultures, influenced by factors such as hierarchy, communication styles, and decision-making processes.

In many Asian cultures, punctuality is highly valued. In Japan and Korea, for instance, it's customary to arrive a few minutes early for meetings. In contrast, in some Southeast Asian countries, a more relaxed attitude towards time may be observed.

The structure of meetings can also differ. In Japan, meetings often begin with small talk and relationship-building before moving on to business matters. Decision-making is typically a consensus-based process that may take place outside of the formal meeting setting.

In China, building relationships (guanxi) is crucial, and significant time may be spent on socializing and getting to know business partners before diving into negotiations. Patience is key, as rushing to close a deal may be seen as aggressive or disrespectful.

In India, meetings may start with casual conversation and chai (tea), and it's not uncommon for meetings to be interrupted by phone calls or other business matters. Flexibility and patience are important.

Across many Asian cultures, it's important to be mindful of hierarchy in meetings. The most senior person on each side often leads the conversation, and it may be considered disrespectful for junior members to speak out of turn or contradict their superiors.

For franchisors and franchisees navigating these diverse meeting cultures, it's important to be observant, flexible, and prepared for different styles of interaction. It's also advisable to clarify expectations regarding meeting structure and decision-making processes in advance.

Dining Etiquette

Business meals play a significant role in relationship-building across many Asian cultures, and understanding local dining etiquette is crucial.

In Japan, formal business dinners often involve multiple courses and can be quite elaborate. It's polite to wait for the host to begin eating and to try a bit of everything that is served. When using chopsticks, it's important never to stick them upright in rice, as this resembles a funeral ritual.

In China, round tables are common for business dinners, with the seat facing the door considered the place of honour. It's customary for the host to order dishes for the entire table. Toasting is an important part of Chinese dining culture, and it's polite to participate, even if just sipping the drink.

In India, it's important to be aware of dietary restrictions, as many people are vegetarian or do not eat beef for religious reasons. Eating with the right hand is customary in traditional settings, though utensils are commonly used in business contexts.

Across many Asian cultures, it's considered polite to leave a small amount of food on your plate to indicate that you have been well-fed. Finishing everything might suggest that you weren't given enough food.

For franchises, understanding these dining customs is crucial not only for building relationships but also for adapting food service concepts to local markets.

Dress Code and Appearance

While business attire in Asia has generally become more westernized, there are still important cultural considerations to keep in mind.

In Japan and Korea, conservative business attire is the norm. Dark suits for men and conservative dresses or suits for women are standard in formal business settings. In Southeast Asian countries like Thailand and Indonesia, business attire may be more relaxed, but it's still important to dress modestly and professionally.

In some countries, traditional dress may be appropriate or even expected in certain business or ceremonial contexts. For example, the

Barong Tagalog in the Philippines or the Sherwani in India might be worn for formal events.

It's also important to be mindful of religious and cultural sensitivities regarding dress. In predominantly Muslim countries like Malaysia and Indonesia, modest dress is appreciated, particularly for women.

For franchises, particularly those in the fashion or service industries, understanding local dress codes and cultural sensitivities is crucial not only for business interactions but also for adapting product offerings and uniforms to local markets.

Navigating Cultural Differences in Business Etiquette

Given the diversity of business etiquette across Asian cultures, franchises must develop strategies to navigate these differences effectively. Some key approaches include:

⇒ Research and Preparation: Before entering a new market, conduct thorough research on local business customs and etiquette. This can include reading cultural guides, attending workshops, or consulting with local experts.

⇒ Cultural Training: Provide comprehensive cultural training for staff at all levels, particularly those who will be interacting with partners, franchisees, or customers in different cultural contexts.

⇒ Local Partnerships: Cultivate relationships with local partners or advisors who can provide insights into cultural nuances and help navigate complex social situations.

⇒ Flexibility and Adaptability: Encourage a mindset of cultural flexibility among franchise staff. The ability to adapt to different cultural norms and expectations is crucial for success in diverse markets.

⇒ Respect and Humility: Approach cultural differences with respect and humility. Showing genuine interest in and respect for local customs can go a long way in building positive relationships.

⇒ Continuous Learning: Recognize that understanding cultural etiquette is an ongoing process. Encourage continuous learning and sharing of experiences within the franchise network.

By understanding and respecting local customs surrounding greetings, gift-giving, meeting conduct, dining, and dress code, franchises can build stronger relationships, avoid costly misunderstandings, and position themselves for success in Asian markets. As the business world becomes increasingly globalized, the ability to navigate these cultural nuances with grace and respect will remain a key differentiator for successful franchise operations in Asia.

Building Relationships

This section explores the nuances of relationship-building across various Asian cultures, highlighting key strategies and considerations for franchisors and franchisees to foster strong, lasting partnerships.

The Significance of Relationships in Asian Business Culture

Across much of Asia, business relationships are not merely transactional; they are deeply personal and often seen as long-term commitments. The concept of relationship-building in business, known as "guanxi" in China, "inhwa" in Korea, or simply "connections" in other parts of Asia, is fundamental to how business is conducted. These relationships often extend beyond the confines of the office and can involve personal interactions, social engagements, and mutual obligations.

For franchises operating in Asian markets, understanding and investing in relationship-building is not just good practice, it's essential for success. Strong relationships can facilitate smoother operations, help navigate bureaucratic challenges, and even provide a competitive edge in crowded markets. However, the approach to building these relationships varies significantly across cultures and requires a nuanced understanding of local customs and expectations.

The Role of Trust and Loyalty

Trust is the cornerstone of business relationships in Asia. In many Asian cultures, trust is not easily given but must be earned over time through consistent actions, reliability, and mutual benefit. Once established, this trust forms the basis of a loyal business relationship that can withstand challenges and create opportunities.

In Japan, for instance, the concept of "nemawashi" involves building consensus through individual conversations before a formal meeting. This process is crucial for establishing trust and ensuring smooth decision-making. In China, trust is often built through repeated social interactions and the fulfilment of mutual obligations.

For franchises, building trust might involve demonstrating long-term commitment to the market, showing respect for local customs and business practices, and being reliable in all dealings. It's important to recognize that in many Asian cultures, trust is given to individuals rather than companies, making personal relationships crucial even in corporate settings.

The Importance of Face and Harmony

The concept of "face" (mianzi in Chinese, mentsu in Japanese) is integral to relationship-building in many Asian cultures. Face refers to a person's reputation, dignity, and prestige. Causing someone to lose face can severely damage relationships, while giving face (through praise, respect, or favours) can strengthen them.

Maintaining harmony in relationships is also highly valued in many Asian cultures. This often translates to avoiding direct confrontation or criticism, particularly in public settings. Instead, disagreements might be handled indirectly or through intermediaries to preserve the relationship and save face for all parties involved.

For franchises, this means being mindful of how feedback is given, how disagreements are handled, and how praise is distributed. It may involve developing more indirect communication strategies and being attuned to subtle cues that indicate discomfort or disagreement.

Relationship-Building Strategies

While specific approaches to relationship-building vary across Asian cultures, several key strategies can be effective across the region:

⇒ Invest Time in Personal Connections: In many Asian cultures, business relationships are built on personal connections. This might involve spending time getting to know partners outside of formal business settings, participating in social activities, or showing interest in local culture and customs.

⇒ Practice Patience: Building strong relationships takes time in Asia. Rushing to close deals or push for quick decisions can be seen as aggressive or disrespectful. Franchises should be prepared to invest time in cultivating relationships before expecting significant business outcomes.

⇒ Demonstrate Long-Term Commitment: Many Asian businesses value long-term partnerships over short-term gains. Franchises can demonstrate their commitment through consistent engagement, long-term planning, and investment in local communities.

⇒ Respect Hierarchy and Status: In many Asian cultures, hierarchy and status play important roles in business relationships. Understanding and respecting these structures is crucial for building effective relationships at all levels of an organization.

⇒ Engage in Reciprocity: The concept of reciprocity is important in many Asian cultures. This doesn't necessarily mean direct quid pro quo, but rather a general understanding of mutual benefit and support over time.

Relationship-Building in Different Asian Contexts

While there are common threads in relationship-building across Asia, it's important to recognize the significant variations between cultures:

In China, the concept of guanxi involves a complex network of relationships and mutual obligations. Building guanxi might involve sharing meals, exchanging gifts (within legal and ethical boundaries), and helping with personal or professional favours. However, it's crucial to navigate this carefully to avoid ethical issues or the appearance of impropriety.

In Japan, relationship-building often involves a more formal process. Initial meetings might be very structured, with a focus on exchanging information rather than making decisions. Building trust often involves demonstrating reliability and attention to detail over time. After-work socializing, known as "nomikai," can play an important role in deepening business relationships.

In Korea, the concept of "jeong" refers to a deep emotional connection that underlies many social and business interactions. Building relationships often involves shared experiences, such as dining together or participating in activities outside of work. The practice of "hoesik," or after-work dining and drinking, is common for building team cohesion and deepening business relationships.

In Southeast Asian countries like Thailand, Malaysia, and Indonesia, relationship-building often involves a more relaxed and personal approach. Showing genuine interest in local culture, participating in social activities, and demonstrating respect for local customs can go a long way in building strong relationships.

In India, relationship-building often involves a blend of professional and personal interactions. It's common for business discussions to be interspersed with personal conversation, and showing interest in Indian culture and traditions is often appreciated. Patience is key, as decision-making processes can be lengthy and involve multiple stakeholders.

Challenges and Considerations

While strong relationships are crucial for success in Asian markets, there are several challenges and considerations that franchises must navigate:

⇒ Ethical Considerations: The line between relationship-building and improper influence can sometimes be blurry. Franchises must be careful to stay within legal and ethical boundaries, particularly when it comes to gift-giving or extending favours.

⇒ Balancing Relationships and Objectivity: Strong personal relationships can sometimes cloud objective business decision-making. Franchises need to find a balance between cultivating strong relationships and maintaining professional objectivity.

⇒ Cultural Differences Within Asia: It's crucial to recognize that relationship-building practices vary not just between Western and Asian cultures, but also among different Asian cultures. What works in China may not be appropriate in Japan or India.

⇒ Time and Resource Investment: Building strong relationships in Asia often requires significant time and resource investment. Franchises need to be prepared for this long-term commitment and allocate resources accordingly.

⇒ Maintaining Relationships Across Distance: For international franchises, maintaining strong relationships across geographical distances can be challenging. Regular communication, periodic visits, and leveraging technology for virtual interactions are important.

Strategies for Effective Relationship-Building in Franchising

For franchises operating in Asian markets, several strategies can be particularly effective for building strong relationships:

⇒ Localization of Leadership: Having local leaders or partners who understand the cultural nuances of relationship-building can be invaluable. These individuals can serve as cultural bridges and help navigate complex social dynamics.

⇒ Comprehensive Cultural Training: Provide thorough cultural training for all staff involved in Asian operations, focusing not just on etiquette but on the deeper cultural values and expectations around relationships.

⇒ Regular Face-to-Face Interactions: While technology has made remote communication easier, face-to-face interactions remain crucial for building trust and deepening relationships in many Asian cultures. Regular visits and in-person meetings should be prioritized.

⇒ Community Engagement: Demonstrating commitment to local communities through corporate social responsibility initiatives or community engagement can help build positive relationships and goodwill.

⇒ Adaptable Communication Strategies: Develop communication strategies that can adapt to different cultural contexts, recognizing that the style and frequency of communication that works in one market may need to be adjusted for another.

⇒ Long-Term Perspective: Approach relationship-building with a long-term perspective, recognizing that the investments made in relationships today may not yield immediate results but can provide significant benefits over time.

Building strong relationships is a critical success factor for franchises operating in Asian markets. By understanding the cultural nuances of relationship-building, investing time and resources in cultivating personal connections, and navigating the challenges with sensitivity and adaptability, franchises can create a strong foundation for sustainable success in the diverse and dynamic business landscape of Asia. As markets continue to evolve and interconnect, the ability to build and maintain strong cross-cultural relationships will remain a key competitive advantage in the franchise industry.

Adapting Products and Services

In the diverse and dynamic markets of Asia, successful franchising often hinges on the ability to adapt products and services to local tastes, preferences, and cultural norms. This section explores the importance of localization, strategies for effective adaptation, and the challenges franchises may face in this process.

The Importance of Localization in Asian Markets

The concept of "one size fits all" rarely applies in the complex tapestry of Asian markets. Each country, and often regions within countries, has its own unique cultural preferences, dietary habits, religious considerations, and consumer behaviours. Franchises that recognize and respond to these differences are more likely to resonate with local consumers and achieve long-term success.

Localization goes beyond mere translation of menus or marketing materials. It involves a deep understanding of local culture, traditions, and consumer psychology. For franchises, this often means reimagining products, services, and even entire business models to align with local expectations while maintaining the essence of the brand.

Understanding Local Consumer Behaviour

The first step in adapting products and services is to gain a thorough understanding of local consumer behaviour. This involves comprehensive market research, including demographic analysis, consumer surveys, focus groups, and observation of local competitors.

In China, for instance, consumers often place high value on brands that convey status and sophistication. This might necessitate adjustments in product positioning or even the introduction of premium lines. In contrast, in markets like India or Indonesia, value for money is often a key consideration, which might require franchises to adapt their pricing strategies or portion sizes.

Understanding local digital trends is also crucial. In South Korea, for example, where digital adoption is extremely high, franchises might need to invest heavily in online ordering systems and digital marketing. In other markets, traditional forms of advertising and in-person experiences might still hold more sway.

Adapting Food and Beverage Offerings

For food and beverage franchises, adapting to local tastes is often the most visible and necessary form of localization. This can involve modifying existing menu items, introducing entirely new products, or adjusting portion sizes and presentation.

In Japan, for example, McDonald's has introduced items like the Teriyaki McBurger and seasonal offerings like the Tsukimi Burger to appeal to local tastes. In India, where a significant portion of the population is vegetarian, many fast-food chains have developed extensive vegetarian menus, with Pizza Hut offering options like Tandoori Paneer pizza.

It's not just about introducing new flavours, but also about understanding local dining habits and preferences. In many Asian countries, for instance, sharing dishes is common, which might require franchises to adjust their serving styles or introduce family-sized portions.

Adapting Retail and Service Offerings

For retail and service franchises, adaptation might involve adjusting product lines, service offerings, or even the entire store concept to meet local needs and preferences.

In the fashion retail sector, this could mean adjusting clothing sizes to fit local body types, offering styles that align with local modesty standards, or introducing products suited to local climates. For example, Uniqlo has developed specific product lines for Southeast Asian markets that cater to the region's tropical climate.

Service franchises might need to adapt their offerings to local customs and expectations. In many Asian countries, for instance, home services are more common than in Western markets, leading some franchises to introduce or expand their home delivery or in-home service options.

Cultural Sensitivity in Product and Service Adaptation

Adapting products and services also requires a high degree of cultural sensitivity. This involves understanding and respecting local cultural norms, religious practices, and superstitions.

For example, in many Asian cultures, certain numbers are considered lucky or unlucky. A hotel franchise might avoid using the number 4 for floor or room numbers in China, as it's associated with death. Similarly, product names or marketing slogans need to be carefully vetted to ensure they don't have unintended negative connotations in local languages.

Religious considerations are also crucial. In Muslim-majority countries like Malaysia and Indonesia, ensuring food products are halal-certified is essential. In India, respecting Hindu sensitivities around beef is crucial for food franchises.

Balancing Global Brand Identity with Local Adaptation

One of the key challenges in adapting products and services is maintaining a consistent global brand identity while catering to local preferences. This requires striking a delicate balance between standardization and localization.

Some elements of the brand, such as core values, quality standards, and key visual identifiers, should remain consistent across markets. However, other elements can be more flexible to allow for local adaptation.

Starbucks, for example, maintains its core brand identity and store aesthetics globally but offers localized menu items in different markets, such as Matcha Frappuccinos in Japan or Bubble Gum Frappuccinos in Indonesia.

Technology and Digital Adaptation

In many Asian markets, particularly in East Asia, adapting to local digital ecosystems is crucial. This might involve integrating with local payment systems, such as WeChat Pay or Alipay in China, or Line Pay in Thailand and Japan.

It may also mean adapting digital ordering systems, loyalty programs, or mobile apps to local preferences and platforms. In South Korea, for instance, where food delivery is highly advanced, franchises might need to integrate with popular local delivery apps or develop their own sophisticated delivery systems.

Pricing and Value Proposition

Adapting products and services often involves rethinking pricing strategies and value propositions. This goes beyond simple currency conversion and involves understanding local economic conditions, competitive landscapes, and consumer expectations around value.

In some markets, this might mean introducing lower-priced options or smaller portion sizes to make products more accessible. In others, it might involve creating premium offerings to cater to a growing middle class or luxury market.

For example, Domino's Pizza in India introduced small, affordably priced pizzas to compete with local street food, while also offering premium options to cater to more affluent consumers.

Packaging and Presentation

Adapting packaging and presentation to local preferences can significantly impact product appeal. This might involve adjusting package sizes, using locally preferred materials, or incorporating cultural elements into the design.

In Japan, for instance, where gift-giving is an important cultural practice, many franchises offer elaborate gift packaging options. In markets where sustainability is a growing concern, franchises might need to adapt their packaging to more eco-friendly alternatives.

Regulatory Compliance and Standards

Adapting products and services also involves ensuring compliance with local regulations and standards. This can include food safety regulations, labelling requirements, or industry-specific standards.

For example, franchises operating in China need to navigate complex regulations around food additives and ingredients. In many Southeast Asian countries, franchises may need to obtain halal certification for their products.

Strategies for Effective Product and Service Adaptation

To effectively adapt products and services for Asian markets, franchises can employ several strategies:

⇒ Comprehensive Market Research: Invest in thorough market research to understand local consumer preferences, cultural norms, and competitive landscapes. This might involve partnering with local research firms or universities.

⇒ Local Partnerships: Collaborate with local partners or franchisees who have deep knowledge of the market. Their insights can be invaluable in identifying opportunities for adaptation.

⇒ Pilot Testing: Before full-scale launches, conduct pilot tests of adapted products or services in select locations. This allows for fine-tuning based on real consumer feedback.

⇒ Continuous Feedback Loop: Establish systems for ongoing customer feedback and market monitoring. Consumer preferences can change rapidly, especially in fast-growing Asian markets.

⇒ Cross-Functional Teams: Create teams that bring together local and global expertise, including marketing, product development, and operations, to ensure adaptations are both locally relevant and aligned with global brand standards.

⇒ Flexible Supply Chains: Develop supply chain flexibility to accommodate local sourcing and production of adapted products.

⇒ Training and Education: Invest in training programs to ensure local staff understand the reasoning behind product adaptations and can effectively communicate this to customers.

Challenges in Product and Service Adaptation

While adapting products and services is crucial, it comes with several challenges:

⇒ Cost Implications: Developing and producing localized products can be costly, especially for smaller markets.

⇒ Quality Control: Maintaining consistent quality across adapted products and services can be challenging, particularly when using local suppliers or ingredients.

⇒ Brand Dilution: Over-adaptation can risk diluting the global brand identity. It's important to maintain core brand elements while adapting others.

⇒ Regulatory Hurdles: Navigating different regulatory environments for adapted products can be complex and time-consuming.

⇒ Speed of Change: Asian markets, particularly in the digital space, can change rapidly. Keeping pace with these changes in product and service offerings can be challenging.

In conclusion, adapting products and services is a critical success factor for franchises operating in Asian markets. It requires a delicate balance between maintaining global brand identity and catering to local preferences. By investing in market research, fostering local partnerships, and maintaining flexibility in product development and operations, franchises can create offerings that resonate with local consumers while staying true to their core brand values. As Asian markets continue to evolve and grow, the ability to effectively adapt products and services will remain a key differentiator in the competitive franchise landscape.

Overcoming Common Challenges

Language Barriers

Language barriers represent one of the most significant challenges for franchises operating in Asian markets. The diverse linguistic landscape of Asia, coupled with varying levels of English proficiency across the region, can create substantial obstacles in communication, operations, and customer relations. This section explores the implications of language barriers and provides strategies for franchises to effectively navigate this challenge.

The Linguistic Landscape of Asia

Asia is home to thousands of languages and dialects, many of which are dominant in their respective countries or regions. While English is widely used in business contexts in some areas, its prevalence and the level of proficiency vary greatly across the continent.

In countries like Singapore and the Philippines, English is an official language and is widely spoken in business settings. However, in markets like Japan, South Korea, and China, despite significant investments in English education, proficiency levels can still present challenges for foreign businesses. In Southeast Asian countries like Thailand, Vietnam, and Indonesia, English proficiency varies widely, often correlating with urban areas and younger generations.

Understanding this linguistic diversity is crucial for franchises, as it impacts every aspect of operations, from staff training to customer interactions and marketing strategies.

Impact on Franchise Operations

Language barriers can affect franchise operations in numerous ways. Effective communication with local franchisees, suppliers, and employees is crucial for successful operations, and language barriers can lead to misunderstandings, delays, and inefficiencies. In many service-oriented franchises, the ability to communicate effectively with customers is paramount, and language barriers can lead to customer dissatisfaction and lost business opportunities.

Marketing and branding also face challenges, as translating marketing materials, slogans, and brand messages requires not just linguistic skills but also cultural understanding to ensure the intended message is conveyed appropriately. Navigating local laws and regulations becomes more challenging when dealing with documents in local languages, and misinterpretation of legal requirements can lead to compliance issues.

Furthermore, effective training of local staff and transfer of operational knowledge can be hindered by language barriers, potentially impacting service quality and brand consistency.

Strategies for Overcoming Language Barriers

To effectively overcome language barriers, franchises can employ a variety of strategies. Investing in language training for both expatriate and local staff can significantly improve communication. This might involve providing English language training to local staff in markets where English is not widely spoken or offering local language training to expatriate staff to help them better integrate with local teams and understand the market. Beyond general language skills, training in business-specific language and cultural communication norms is crucial.

For critical communications, relying on professional translation and interpretation services is often necessary. This is particularly important for legal documents, marketing materials, and training resources. Ensuring all contracts, franchise agreements, and regulatory filings are professionally translated can help avoid legal misunderstandings. Accurate translation of operational manuals and training materials is crucial for maintaining consistent standards across markets.

Creating multilingual resources can help bridge language gaps. Developing websites and mobile applications in relevant local languages can improve accessibility for customers and local partners. Creating bilingual versions of key operational documents, manuals, and training materials can also be beneficial. Utilizing visual aids, infographics, and videos to complement written materials can make information more accessible across language barriers.

Modern technology offers various tools to assist in overcoming language barriers. While not suitable for formal business communications, translation apps can be helpful for day-to-day interactions. Providing staff with access to language learning software can support ongoing language development. In some customer service settings, real-time translation devices can facilitate communication with customers.

Building a diverse team with multilingual capabilities can be a significant asset. Prioritizing the hiring of local staff with the necessary language skills can help bridge communication gaps. Considering language skills as a key factor in recruitment and promotion decisions can strengthen the organization's linguistic capabilities. Developing a leadership team that reflects the linguistic diversity of the markets in which the franchise operates can enhance overall communication effectiveness.

Adapting Communication Styles

Beyond language itself, franchises must also consider adapting communication styles to suit local norms. Many Asian cultures tend towards high-context communication, where much is implied rather than explicitly stated. This contrasts with the more direct, low-context communication style common in many Western cultures. Understanding and adapting to local norms in non-verbal communication, such as body language and facial expressions, is crucial. Communication styles in many Asian cultures are influenced by hierarchical structures and formality, and understanding these nuances is important for effective communication.

Localizing Customer-Facing Elements

For franchises dealing directly with customers, localizing customer-facing elements is crucial. This includes ensuring menus and product descriptions are accurately translated and culturally appropriate. All in-store signage, including directional signs and promotional materials, should be in the local language. Developing customer service scripts and training in local languages can ensure staff can effectively assist customers.

Managing Expectations and Building Patience

Overcoming language barriers is an ongoing process that requires patience and realistic expectations. It's important to recognize that communication across language barriers may take longer and to factor this into project timelines and expectations. Fostering an organizational culture that values patience and understanding in cross-linguistic communications can help manage frustrations. Recognizing and celebrating improvements in cross-linguistic communication can encourage ongoing efforts.

Legal and Compliance Considerations

In dealing with language barriers, franchises must be particularly careful in legal and compliance matters. Engaging local legal experts who are fluent in both the local language and the franchise's primary language can ensure accurate interpretation of legal requirements. When possible, creating bilingual versions of contracts and legal documents, specifying which language version takes precedence in case of discrepancies, can provide additional clarity. Ensuring all regulatory communications and filings are accurately translated and comply with local language requirements is essential for maintaining legal compliance.

While language barriers present significant challenges for franchises operating in Asian markets, they are not insurmountable. By implementing a comprehensive strategy that includes language training, professional translation services, technological solutions, and cultural adaptation, franchises can effectively navigate these challenges. Moreover, successfully overcoming language barriers can become a competitive advantage, allowing franchises to connect more deeply with local markets and build stronger relationships with partners and customers. As Asia continues to be a key growth region for global franchises, the ability to effectively manage and overcome language barriers will remain a critical skill for franchise success in the region.

Bureaucracy and Red Tape

Bureaucracy and red tape are often cited as significant hurdles for businesses operating in many Asian markets. The complex web of regulations, administrative procedures, and governmental oversight can present formidable challenges for franchises seeking to establish and expand their operations in the region. This section delves into the nature of these challenges and offers strategies for navigating the often-intricate bureaucratic landscapes of Asian markets.

Understanding Bureaucracy in Asian Markets

Bureaucracy in Asian markets is often characterized by a complex interplay of historical, cultural, and political factors. Many Asian countries have long-standing traditions of centralized governance, which can result in elaborate administrative systems. Additionally, the rapid economic growth experienced by many Asian nations in recent decades has led to the development of regulatory frameworks that aim to manage this growth, sometimes resulting in layers of overlapping regulations.

It's important to note that the level and nature of bureaucracy can vary significantly across different Asian countries. For instance, Singapore is often praised for its efficient and business-friendly bureaucracy, while countries like India or Indonesia may present more complex regulatory environments. Understanding these variations is crucial for franchises operating across multiple Asian markets.

Business Registration and Licensing

One of the primary areas where franchises encounter bureaucratic hurdles is in the process of business registration and licensing. This process can be particularly complex for foreign businesses, often involving multiple government agencies and requiring numerous documents and approvals. In some countries, the requirements may vary depending on the specific sector or type of business activity.

For example, in China, foreign businesses often need to navigate a multi-step process involving several government bodies, including the

Ministry of Commerce, the State Administration for Industry and Commerce, and local government offices. The process can be time-consuming and may require multiple rounds of document submission and review.

Regulatory Compliance

Ongoing regulatory compliance is another area where bureaucracy can pose significant challenges. Many Asian countries have strict regulations governing various aspects of business operations, from labour laws and environmental standards to food safety regulations and advertising guidelines. These regulations can be complex and subject to frequent changes, requiring businesses to stay constantly vigilant and adaptable.

In Japan, for instance, the regulatory environment is known for its thoroughness and attention to detail. Businesses may need to comply with numerous industry-specific regulations, which can be particularly challenging for franchises operating in sectors like food and beverage or healthcare.

Tax Systems and Financial Reporting

Navigating tax systems and meeting financial reporting requirements can be another bureaucratic challenge in many Asian markets. Tax regulations can be complex, with different levels of taxation (national, regional, local) and various types of taxes to consider. Financial reporting requirements may be stringent, often requiring detailed documentation and adherence to specific accounting standards.

In India, the introduction of the Goods and Services Tax (GST) in 2017 aimed to simplify the tax structure, but the implementation process presented its own set of bureaucratic challenges for businesses, including franchises.

Import and Export Procedures

For franchises that rely on importing products or materials, dealing with customs and import procedures can be a significant source of bureaucratic friction. Many Asian countries have complex import regulations, including tariffs, quotas, and product standards that must be met. The paperwork and inspections involved can lead to delays and increased costs.

Similarly, franchises looking to export products from their Asian operations may face bureaucratic hurdles in the form of export licenses, certificates of origin, and compliance with international trade agreements.

Strategies for Navigating Bureaucracy and Red Tape

While the bureaucratic challenges in Asian markets can be daunting, there are several strategies that franchises can employ to navigate these complexities more effectively.

Develop Local Expertise

One of the most crucial strategies for dealing with bureaucracy is to develop strong local expertise. This can involve hiring local staff with experience in navigating the regulatory environment or partnering with local consultants or law firms. These local experts can provide invaluable insights into the nuances of bureaucratic processes and can often facilitate smoother interactions with government agencies.

For instance, a franchise entering the Korean market might benefit from hiring a local regulatory affairs specialist who understands the intricacies of the country's business regulations and has established relationships with relevant government departments.

Build Relationships with Regulatory Bodies

In many Asian cultures, personal relationships play a significant role in business dealings, including interactions with government agencies. While it's crucial to maintain ethical standards and avoid any appearance of impropriety, building professional relationships with key regulatory officials can be beneficial. This might involve attending industry events where government representatives are present, participating in public-private dialogue forums, or engaging in corporate social responsibility initiatives that align with government priorities.

Leverage Technology and Digital Solutions

As many Asian countries modernize their bureaucratic processes, there are increasing opportunities to leverage technology to streamline compliance and administrative tasks. This might involve using e-government portals for business registration or tax filing, implementing software solutions for regulatory compliance management, or utilizing digital platforms for customs declarations.

In Singapore, for example, the government's commitment to digital transformation has resulted in user-friendly online platforms for various business-related processes, significantly reducing the bureaucratic burden on companies.

Prioritize Transparency and Documentation

Given the complexity of many bureaucratic processes in Asian markets, maintaining meticulous records and prioritizing transparency in all dealings with government agencies is crucial. This involves keeping detailed documentation of all interactions, decisions, and compliance efforts. Having a clear paper trail can be invaluable in demonstrating compliance and resolving any disputes that may arise.

Stay Informed About Regulatory Changes

The regulatory landscape in many Asian countries is dynamic, with frequent changes and updates to rules and procedures. Franchises need to stay informed about these changes and be prepared to adapt their practices accordingly. This might involve subscribing to government newsletters, participating in industry associations, or engaging legal counsel to provide regular regulatory updates.

Plan for Bureaucratic Delays

When planning business activities in Asian markets, it's important to factor in potential bureaucratic delays. This might mean starting application processes well in advance of planned activities or building buffer time into project timelines to account for potential administrative holdups.

Consider Regional Variations

For franchises operating across multiple Asian countries, it's important to recognize that bureaucratic challenges can vary significantly from one market to another. A one-size-fits-all approach is unlikely to be effective. Instead, developing market-specific strategies for dealing with bureaucracy, while maintaining overall corporate standards, can be more successful.

Case Study: Navigating Bureaucracy in Indonesia

Indonesia, Southeast Asia's largest economy, presents a compelling case study in navigating bureaucracy. The country has made significant strides in recent years to improve its business environment, but bureaucratic challenges remain.

One major initiative has been the development of the Online Single Submission (OSS) system, launched in 2018. This system aims to streamline business licensing processes by providing a single portal for various permits and licenses. However, the implementation of this system has not been without challenges, and businesses still often need to navigate complex procedures at both the national and local levels.

A successful franchise operating in Indonesia might employ a multi-faceted approach to dealing with bureaucracy:

⇒ Engaging local partners or consultants with expertise in navigating the OSS system and other regulatory processes.
⇒ Maintaining strong relationships with both national and local government officials, recognizing the significant role that regional authorities play in many regulatory matters.
⇒ Staying actively involved in industry associations that can provide updates on regulatory changes and collectively advocate for business-friendly reforms.

⇒ Investing in robust compliance management systems to ensure adherence to the country's complex and sometimes overlapping regulations.

⇒ Building flexibility into business plans to account for potential bureaucratic delays, particularly in areas like import procedures or local level permitting.

The Future of Bureaucracy in Asian Markets

While bureaucratic challenges remain significant in many Asian markets, it's important to note that many countries in the region are actively working to streamline their administrative processes and improve their business environments. Initiatives like regulatory guillotines (systematic reviews to eliminate unnecessary regulations), e-government solutions, and investment in public sector capacity building are becoming increasingly common.

Franchises operating in Asia should stay attuned to these developments and be prepared to adapt their strategies as bureaucratic landscapes evolve. At the same time, they should continue to invest in building the relationships, local knowledge, and compliance capabilities necessary to navigate the complex regulatory environments that are likely to persist, to some degree, in many Asian markets for the foreseeable future.

By developing a deep understanding of local regulatory environments, building strong relationships, leveraging technology, and maintaining flexibility, franchises can effectively navigate these challenges. Moreover, those that excel in managing bureaucratic complexities may find that they have developed a valuable competitive advantage in these dynamic and growing markets.

Competition from Local Brands

As international franchises expand into Asian markets, they often face stiff competition from well-established local brands. These homegrown competitors possess intimate knowledge of local consumer preferences, cultural nuances, and market dynamics, giving them a significant advantage. This section explores the challenges posed by local brand competition and provides strategies for international franchises to effectively compete and thrive in Asian markets.

Understanding the Strength of Local Brands

Local brands in Asian markets have several inherent advantages that make them formidable competitors. These advantages stem from their deep-rooted understanding of local culture, long-standing presence in the market, and ability to quickly adapt to changing consumer preferences.

Cultural Resonance

One of the primary strengths of local brands is their cultural resonance. These brands often have a long history in their home markets and have built strong emotional connections with consumers over time. They understand local traditions, values, and social norms, allowing them to create marketing messages and product offerings that deeply resonate with local consumers.

For example, in China, local beverage brand Wahaha has successfully leveraged its understanding of Chinese cultural values and preferences to build a strong brand identity. Its marketing campaigns often tap into themes of family, tradition, and national pride, which resonate strongly with Chinese consumers.

Market Knowledge and Agility

Local brands typically possess an intimate understanding of local market dynamics, including consumer behaviour, distribution channels, and regulatory environments. This knowledge allows them to be more agile in responding to market changes and consumer trends.

In India, for instance, local fast-food chain Jumbo King has successfully competed against international burger franchises by offering vada pav, a popular local street food, in a quick-service restaurant format. The brand's understanding of local taste preferences and eating habits has allowed it to carve out a significant market share.

Price Competitiveness

Local brands often have the advantage of lower operational costs, allowing them to offer products at more competitive prices. This can be particularly challenging for international franchises that may have higher overhead costs due to import taxes, expatriate salaries, or royalty fees.

Nationalist Sentiment

In some Asian markets, there is a growing trend of consumer nationalism, where customers prefer local brands as a way of supporting the domestic economy. This sentiment can pose a significant challenge for international franchises trying to establish themselves in these markets.

Challenges Faced by International Franchises

Adapting to Local Tastes

One of the primary challenges for international franchises is adapting their products or services to local tastes while maintaining brand consistency. This balancing act can be particularly difficult in markets with strong culinary traditions or unique consumer preferences.

Building Brand Awareness and Trust

In markets where local brands have a long-standing presence, international franchises often struggle to build brand awareness and trust. Consumers may be hesitant to try unfamiliar brands, particularly if they perceive them as being more expensive or less attuned to local preferences.

Navigating Local Business Practices

International franchises may find it challenging to navigate local business practices, including relationships with suppliers, landlords, and government officials. Local brands often have well-established networks and understand the nuances of doing business in their home markets.

Competing on Price

As mentioned earlier, local brands often have a cost advantage that allows them to offer more competitive pricing. International franchises may struggle to match these prices while maintaining their quality standards and profit margins.

Strategies for Competing with Local Brands

Despite these challenges, international franchises can implement several strategies to effectively compete with local brands in Asian markets.

Localization with Global Standards

One of the most effective strategies is to localize offerings while maintaining global quality standards. This approach involves adapting products, services, and marketing strategies to local preferences while leveraging the franchise's international reputation for quality and consistency.

For example, McDonald's has successfully implemented this strategy in many Asian markets. In India, the company has developed a menu that caters to local tastes, including items like the McAloo Tikki burger, while maintaining its global standards for food safety and service quality.

Leveraging Global Brand Equity

While local brands may have strong cultural resonance, international franchises can leverage their global brand equity. Many consumers in Asian markets associate international brands with prestige, quality, and modernity. Franchises can capitalize on this perception by highlighting their global presence and international standards in their marketing communications.

Starbucks, for instance, has successfully positioned itself as a premium, aspirational brand in many Asian markets, appealing to consumers who seek a global coffee experience.

Innovation and Differentiation

International franchises can compete by offering innovative products or services that are not available from local competitors. This could involve introducing new technologies, unique service concepts, or product innovations that set the franchise apart from local offerings.

In Japan, Domino's Pizza has differentiated itself from local pizza chains by focusing on delivery service and digital ordering technologies, areas where many local competitors were lagging.

Strategic Partnerships and Collaborations

Forming partnerships with local companies or brands can help international franchises navigate the market more effectively. These partnerships can provide valuable local knowledge, help in adapting to local tastes, and potentially mitigate some of the "foreign brand" perceptions.

For example, in China, Starbucks' partnership with local food and beverage giant Tingyi has helped the company expand its ready-to-drink coffee products in the market, leveraging Tingyi's extensive distribution network and local market knowledge.

Investing in Local Talent and Suppliers

By investing in local talent and working with local suppliers, international franchises can deepen their understanding of the market and build stronger local connections. This approach can also help in creating a more authentic local presence and potentially reduce costs.

Emphasizing Corporate Social Responsibility

Engaging in meaningful corporate social responsibility (CSR) initiatives can help international franchises build goodwill and connect with local communities. This can be particularly effective in countering perceptions of the franchise as an "outsider" brand.

For instance, Yum! Brands (parent company of KFC, Pizza Hut, and Taco Bell) has implemented various CSR programs in its Asian markets, including hunger relief efforts and education initiatives, which have helped strengthen its brand image.

Leveraging Digital Platforms

Utilizing digital platforms and social media can be an effective way for international franchises to connect with younger consumers and build brand awareness. Many Asian markets have high rates of digital adoption, providing opportunities for innovative marketing and customer engagement strategies.

Case Study: Competing with Local Brands in South Korea

South Korea presents an interesting case study in competing with local brands. The market is known for its strong domestic companies and discerning consumers who often prefer local products.

When Taco Bell entered the South Korean market, it faced stiff competition from local fast-food chains and a consumer base unfamiliar with Mexican cuisine. The company implemented a multi-faceted strategy to compete effectively:

⇒ Menu Localization: Taco Bell introduced items tailored to Korean tastes, such as the Kimchi Quesadilla, while maintaining its core menu offerings.
⇒ Premium Positioning: The company positioned itself as a premium Western dining experience, differentiating from local fast-food chains.
⇒ Digital Innovation: Taco Bell invested heavily in digital ordering and delivery services, catering to Korea's tech-savvy consumers.
⇒ Collaboration with Local Brands: The company partnered with local beverage brands to create unique drink offerings that appealed to Korean consumers.

⇒ Engaging Marketing: Taco Bell used social media influencers and creative campaigns to build brand awareness and educate consumers about Mexican cuisine.

Through these strategies, Taco Bell has managed to establish a growing presence in the competitive South Korean market, demonstrating that international franchises can successfully compete with local brands when they adapt thoughtfully to the local context.

The Evolving Landscape of Brand Competition

As Asian markets continue to develop and globalize, the dynamics of competition between international franchises and local brands are likely to evolve. Increasingly, we may see a blurring of lines between "local" and "global" as local brands expand internationally and global brands become more localized.

International franchises operating in Asia should stay attuned to these changing dynamics. This may involve continually reassessing competitive strategies, staying open to new forms of collaboration or partnership, and remaining agile in response to shifting consumer preferences and market conditions.

Moreover, as consumers in many Asian markets become more globally minded, particularly among younger generations, there may be opportunities for international franchises to position themselves as bridges between local and global cultures. This could involve creating unique fusion products or experiences that blend international and local elements in innovative ways.

In conclusion, while competition from local brands presents significant challenges for international franchises in Asian markets, it also pushes these franchises to innovate, adapt, and ultimately create more compelling offerings for local consumers. By thoughtfully balancing localization with global brand strengths, leveraging innovation and digital technologies, and building meaningful connections with local communities, international franchises can not only compete effectively with local brands but also contribute to the rich and dynamic consumer landscapes of Asian markets.

Maintaining Brand Consistency

Maintaining brand consistency while adapting to local preferences and regulations is a delicate balancing act. This challenge is particularly pronounced in Asia, where cultural diversity, varying consumer behaviours, and differing regulatory environments can necessitate significant adaptations to a franchise's standard operating procedures. This section explores the complexities of maintaining brand consistency in Asian markets and provides strategies for franchises to navigate this challenge effectively.

Understanding the Importance of Brand Consistency

Brand consistency is crucial for franchises as it helps maintain brand recognition, builds trust with consumers, and ensures a uniform customer experience across different locations. A consistent brand image communicates reliability and quality, which are particularly important when entering new markets where the brand may not be well-known.

However, brand consistency goes beyond just visual elements like logos and colour schemes. It encompasses the entire customer experience, including product quality, service standards, store ambiance, and brand values. For franchises, consistency also extends to operational procedures, supplier relationships, and franchisee management.

Challenges to Brand Consistency in Asian Markets

Cultural Differences

One of the primary challenges to maintaining brand consistency in Asia is the vast cultural diversity across the region. What works in one Asian country may not necessarily translate well to another. This diversity affects everything from consumer preferences and buying behaviours to communication styles and service expectations.

For example, a casual dining franchise that emphasizes individual portions and quick turnover in its Western markets might need to adapt to the family-style dining preferences common in many Asian cultures. This adaptation could affect not just the menu but also the restaurant layout, service style, and overall dining experience.

Local Regulations and Standards

Varying regulations and standards across different Asian countries can force franchises to make changes that may impact brand consistency. These could include food safety regulations, labelling requirements, advertising restrictions, or employment laws.

In some cases, these regulations may require significant changes to products or services. For instance, a fast-food franchise might need to reformulate its signature sauce to comply with local food additive regulations, potentially affecting the taste that customers associate with the brand.

Supply Chain Variations

Differences in local supply chains can also pose challenges to brand consistency. Franchises may need to source ingredients or materials locally due to import restrictions, cost considerations, or quality control issues. This can potentially lead to variations in product taste, quality, or appearance.

Language and Communication

Language differences across Asian markets can impact brand consistency in marketing communications, packaging, and customer service interactions. Translating brand slogans, product names, or marketing messages while maintaining their original meaning and brand voice can be challenging.

Local Competition and Market Pressures

Pressure to compete with local brands may tempt franchises to make significant adaptations that could potentially dilute brand consistency. The need to offer locally relevant products or services while maintaining the core brand identity can be a difficult balance to strike.

Strategies for Maintaining Brand Consistency

Despite these challenges, there are several strategies that franchises can employ to maintain brand consistency while successfully adapting to Asian markets.

Develop Clear Brand Guidelines

Creating comprehensive brand guidelines is crucial for maintaining consistency across different markets. These guidelines should cover not just visual elements like logos and colour schemes, but also brand voice, customer service standards, store layouts, and operational procedures.

Importantly, these guidelines should also include parameters for acceptable local adaptations. This provides franchisees with a clear framework for making necessary changes while ensuring that core brand elements remain consistent.

Implement a "Glocal" Approach

A "glocal" approach – combining global brand standards with local market adaptations – can help franchises maintain consistency while still resonating with local consumers. This approach involves identifying core brand elements that must remain consistent across all markets, while allowing flexibility in areas where local adaptation is necessary or beneficial.

For example, a coffee shop franchise might maintain consistent global standards for coffee quality and preparation methods, while allowing flexibility in food menu items to cater to local tastes. This ensures that the core brand promise (high-quality coffee) remains consistent, while still offering locally relevant products.

Invest in Training and Support

Thorough training programs for local franchisees and staff are essential for maintaining brand consistency. These programs should cover not just operational procedures, but also the brand's values, culture, and customer service philosophy.

Ongoing support and regular audits can help ensure that brand standards are consistently maintained. This could include periodic visits from corporate teams, mystery shopper programs, or peer review systems among franchisees.

Leverage Technology for Consistency

Technology can play a crucial role in maintaining brand consistency across different markets. This could include:

⇒ Centralized digital asset management systems to ensure all franchisees have access to up-to-date, approved brand materials.
⇒ Customer relationship management (CRM) systems to maintain consistent customer interactions across different touchpoints.
⇒ Quality control systems to monitor product consistency across different locations.

Carefully Manage Supply Chains

While local sourcing may be necessary in some cases, franchises should strive to maintain consistency in key ingredients or materials that are central to their brand identity. This might involve working closely with local suppliers to ensure they can meet the franchise's quality standards or setting up regional distribution centres to supply key items to multiple markets.

Conduct Regular Brand Audits

Regular brand audits across different Asian markets can help franchises identify any inconsistencies and address them promptly. These audits should assess not just visual brand elements, but also product quality, customer experience, and adherence to operational standards.

Foster a Strong Franchise Culture

Building a strong franchise culture that emphasizes the importance of brand consistency can help ensure that local teams are committed to maintaining brand standards. This involves clear communication of brand values and regular engagement with franchisees to reinforce the importance of consistency.

Case Study: Maintaining Brand Consistency in Japan

Japan provides an interesting case study in maintaining brand consistency due to its unique cultural preferences and high standards for quality and service.

When Subway entered the Japanese market, it faced several challenges in maintaining its brand consistency while adapting to local preferences. The company implemented a multi-faceted approach:

⇒ Menu Adaptation: While maintaining its core submarine sandwich concept, Subway introduced locally relevant options like a shrimp avocado sandwich and a sandwich with teriyaki chicken.

⇒ Service Standards: Subway adapted its service style to meet Japan's high standards for customer service, including more formal greetings and meticulous presentation.

⇒ Store Design: While maintaining key brand elements, Subway adjusted its store designs to suit Japanese preferences for cleaner, more minimalist aesthetics.

⇒ Quality Control: Subway implemented stringent quality control measures to meet Japan's high food safety standards, which also helped maintain consistent product quality.

⇒ Marketing: The company adapted its marketing messages to resonate with Japanese consumers, emphasizing the freshness and health benefits of its products.

Throughout these adaptations, Subway maintained consistency in its core brand elements – the submarine sandwich concept, the ability to customize orders, and its positioning as a healthier fast-food option. This balanced approach allowed Subway to establish a strong presence in the Japanese market while maintaining its global brand identity.

The Future of Brand Consistency in Asian Markets

As Asian markets continue to evolve and become more interconnected, the challenge of maintaining brand consistency while adapting to local needs is likely to become more complex. Franchises will need to become increasingly sophisticated in their approach to brand management, potentially leveraging advanced technologies like artificial intelligence and data analytics to monitor and maintain brand consistency across diverse markets.

Moreover, as consumers in Asian markets become more globally minded, there may be opportunities for franchises to strengthen their global brand identity while still offering locally relevant experiences. This could involve creating unique "fusion" experiences that blend global brand elements with local cultural touchpoints in innovative ways.

The rise of social media and digital platforms also presents both challenges and opportunities for brand consistency. While these platforms can quickly amplify any inconsistencies in brand experience, they also offer franchises powerful tools for communicating their brand identity and values directly to consumers across different markets.

In conclusion, maintaining brand consistency in Asian markets is a complex but crucial task for international franchises. By developing clear brand guidelines, implementing a "glocal" approach, investing in training and technology, and remaining attuned to local market dynamics, franchises can successfully maintain their brand integrity while adapting to the diverse and dynamic markets of Asia. The franchises that master this balance will be well-positioned to build strong, recognizable brands that resonate with consumers across this fast-growing region.

Future Trends in Asian Franchising

Emerging Markets

As the landscape of Asian franchising continues to evolve, several emerging markets are poised to play increasingly significant roles in the future of the industry. These markets present both exciting opportunities and unique challenges for franchisors looking to expand their footprint in Asia. This section explores some of the key emerging markets in the region, their characteristics, and the potential they hold for the franchising sector.

Vietnam: The Rising Star

Vietnam has emerged as one of the most promising markets for franchising in Southeast Asia. With a young, growing population, increasing urbanization, and a rapidly expanding middle class, Vietnam offers fertile ground for franchise expansion.

Market Characteristics

Vietnam's economy has been one of the fastest growing in Asia, with a consistent GDP growth rate averaging around 6-7% annually in recent years. This economic growth has led to increased consumer spending and a hunger for international brands, particularly in urban centres like Ho Chi Minh City and Hanoi.

The country's demographic profile is particularly favourable for franchising. With over 70% of its population under the age of 35, Vietnam boasts a young, tech-savvy consumer base that is eager to try new products and experiences. This demographic is also increasingly brand conscious and willing to pay for quality and convenience.

Opportunities and Challenges

Food and beverage franchises have seen particular success in Vietnam, with both international and local brands expanding rapidly. Retail, education, and service-based franchises are also gaining traction as the country's service sector continues to grow.

However, franchisors entering Vietnam must navigate several challenges. These include complex regulations around foreign ownership, the need for strong local partnerships, and the importance of adapting to local tastes and preferences. Intellectual property protection can also be a concern, necessitating careful legal planning and ongoing vigilance.

Despite these challenges, many franchisors view Vietnam as a key growth market for the coming decades. Those who can successfully navigate the regulatory landscape and tailor their offerings to local preferences are likely to find significant opportunities in this dynamic market.

Indonesia: The Sleeping Giant

As the world's fourth most populous country and Southeast Asia's largest economy, Indonesia represents a massive potential market for franchising. While the franchise sector in Indonesia is not as developed as in some neighbouring countries, it is growing rapidly and attracting increasing interest from both domestic and international franchisors.

Market Characteristics

Indonesia's vast archipelago, with over 17,000 islands, presents both opportunities and challenges for franchisors. The country's diverse population of over 270 million people offers a large consumer base, but also necessitates careful consideration of regional differences in tastes, preferences, and purchasing power.

Like Vietnam, Indonesia benefits from a young demographic profile, with a median age of just 30 years. The country's middle class is expanding rapidly, particularly in urban areas, driving increased consumer spending and demand for modern retail and dining experiences.

Opportunities and Challenges

Food and beverage franchises have been at the forefront of franchise growth in Indonesia, with both international quick-service restaurants and local concepts expanding rapidly. Retail franchises, particularly in the convenience store sector, have also seen significant growth. There's also increasing potential for service-based franchises in areas such as education, healthcare, and personal services.

However, franchisors looking to enter Indonesia must navigate a complex regulatory environment. The country's franchise regulations require franchisors to have at least five years of profitable operations and to use at least 80% local content in their products. These regulations are designed to protect local businesses and ensure technology transfer, but they can pose challenges for international franchisors.

Cultural sensitivity is also crucial in Indonesia, the world's largest Muslim-majority country. Franchisors need to be mindful of religious and cultural norms, particularly in food and beverage concepts.

Despite these challenges, many franchisors see Indonesia as a key long-term growth market. Its large population, growing middle class, and increasing urbanization make it an attractive prospect for franchisors willing to invest the time and resources to understand and adapt to the local market.

Bangladesh: The Next Frontier

Often overlooked in discussions of Asian franchising, Bangladesh is emerging as a potentially significant market for the future. With a population of over 160 million and one of the fastest-growing economies in Asia, Bangladesh is attracting increasing attention from international franchisors.

Market Characteristics

Bangladesh's economy has been growing at an impressive rate, averaging around 6-7% annual GDP growth over the past decade. This growth has led to a gradual expansion of the middle class, particularly in urban areas like Dhaka and Chittagong.

The country's demographic profile is favourable for franchising, with a young population (median age of 27.6 years) and increasing urbanization. As more Bangladeshis move to cities and enter the formal workforce, demand for modern retail and dining experiences is growing.

Opportunities and Challenges

The franchise sector in Bangladesh is still in its early stages, which presents both opportunities and challenges. Food and beverage franchises, particularly quick-service restaurants, have been among the first to enter the market, with several international brands establishing a presence in recent years.

There's also growing potential for retail franchises, particularly in the fashion and accessories sectors, as well as service-based franchises in areas like education and healthcare.

However, franchisors entering Bangladesh face several challenges. The country's infrastructure is still developing, which can pose logistical challenges. The regulatory environment for franchising is not as well-established as in more mature markets, which can create uncertainty. Additionally, adapting to local tastes and preferences is crucial, as Bangladeshi consumers have strong local food traditions and preferences.

Despite these challenges, many franchisors see Bangladesh as a potentially significant market for the future. Its large population, improving economic conditions, and relatively untapped market present opportunities for franchisors willing to take a long-term view and invest in understanding the local market dynamics.

Central Asian Republics: The New Frontier

The Central Asian republics – Kazakhstan, Uzbekistan, Kyrgyzstan, Tajikistan, and Turkmenistan – represent an emerging frontier for franchising in Asia. While these markets are still relatively small and underdeveloped compared to many other Asian countries, they are attracting increasing interest from franchisors looking for new growth opportunities.

Market Characteristics

The Central Asian republics vary significantly in terms of population size, economic development, and openness to foreign investment. Kazakhstan, the largest economy in the region, has been the most receptive to international franchises, particularly in its largest city, Almaty. Uzbekistan, with the largest population in the region, has been gradually opening up its economy and attracting more foreign investment.

These markets are characterized by young populations, growing urbanization, and increasing consumer spending power, particularly in major cities. However, they also face challenges including political instability, underdeveloped infrastructure, and complex regulatory environments.

Opportunities and Challenges

Food and beverage franchises have been among the first to enter Central Asian markets, with several international quick-service restaurant chains establishing a presence, particularly in Kazakhstan and Uzbekistan. There's also growing potential for retail franchises and service-based franchises in areas like education and fitness.

However, franchisors entering these markets face several challenges. These include navigating complex and sometimes opaque regulatory environments, dealing with underdeveloped supply chains, and adapting to local tastes and cultural norms. The need for strong local partnerships is particularly crucial in these markets.

Despite these challenges, some franchisors see the Central Asian republics as potentially significant long-term growth markets. Their strategic location between Europe and Asia, young populations, and gradually improving economic conditions make them interesting prospects for franchisors willing to take a pioneering approach.

The Future of Emerging Markets in Asian Franchising

As we look to the future of franchising in Asia, emerging markets are likely to play an increasingly important role. While more developed markets like China, Japan, and South Korea will continue to be significant, emerging markets offer new frontiers for growth and expansion.

Several trends are likely to shape the development of franchising in these emerging markets:

⇒ Digital Transformation: The rapid adoption of digital technologies in many emerging markets is likely to accelerate the growth of franchising. E-commerce, mobile ordering, and digital payment systems are becoming increasingly prevalent, creating new opportunities for franchisors to reach and serve customers.

⇒ Local Adaptation: Successful franchisors in emerging markets will need to strike a careful balance between maintaining brand consistency and adapting to local preferences and cultural norms. This may involve developing market-specific products or services or adapting existing offerings to local tastes.

⇒ Sustainability and Social Responsibility: As consumers in emerging markets become more environmentally and socially conscious, franchisors will need to demonstrate their commitment to sustainability and corporate social responsibility.

⇒ Rise of Local Franchisors: While international franchisors are likely to continue expanding into emerging markets, we're also likely to see the rise of more local and regional franchise concepts. These home-grown franchises may be better positioned to understand and cater to local preferences.

⇒ Regulatory Evolution: As the franchise sector grows in emerging markets, we're likely to see the evolution of more comprehensive franchise regulations. This could provide greater clarity and protection for both franchisors and franchisees but may also create new compliance challenges.

Emerging markets represent both significant opportunities and unique challenges for franchisors in Asia. Success in these markets will require careful market research, strategic planning, and a willingness to adapt and innovate. Franchisors who can navigate these complex environments and build strong local partnerships are likely to find substantial growth opportunities in the dynamic and diverse emerging markets of Asia.

Sector-specific Opportunities

These sector-specific opportunities are shaped by changing consumer preferences, technological advancements, and broader socioeconomic trends across the region. This section explores some of the key sectors that are likely to offer significant opportunities for franchisors in the coming years.

Health and Wellness

The health and wellness sector are poised for substantial growth in Asian franchising, driven by increasing health consciousness among consumers and a growing middle class with disposable income to spend on personal well-being.

Fitness and Exercise

Fitness franchises are experiencing rapid growth across Asia, with concepts ranging from traditional gyms to boutique fitness studios gaining popularity. The rise of fitness-conscious millennials and Gen Z consumers is fuelling this trend, particularly in urban areas.

One notable trend is the increasing popularity of 24-hour gyms, which cater to the busy lifestyles of urban professionals. These gyms often operate with minimal staffing, leveraging technology for access control and member management, making them an attractive franchise model.

Boutique fitness concepts, such as specialized yoga studios, cycling studios, and high-intensity interval training (HIIT) facilities, are also gaining traction. These niche concepts often foster a sense of community among members, which can lead to high retention rates and strong brand loyalty.

Virtual and hybrid fitness models, which gained popularity during the COVID-19 pandemic, are likely to remain relevant. Franchises that can offer a seamless blend of in-person and virtual fitness experiences may find particular success.

Healthy Eating

The healthy eating sector presents significant opportunities for franchising in Asia. As awareness of the link between diet and health grows, consumers are increasingly seeking out healthier food options.

Fast-casual restaurant concepts that offer nutritious, customizable meals are likely to see continued growth. This includes salad bars, poke bowl restaurants, and health-focused smoothie and juice bars.

There's also growing potential for franchises that cater to specific dietary preferences, such as vegetarian, vegan, or gluten-free options. As these diets become more mainstream in Asia, franchises that can offer tasty, convenient options for these consumers are likely to find success.

Meal prep and healthy food delivery franchises represent another area of opportunity. As busy urban professionals seek convenient ways to maintain healthy diets, franchises that can offer pre-prepared healthy meals or meal kits for home cooking are likely to find a receptive market.

Wellness Services

Beyond fitness and nutrition, there's growing demand for a wide range of wellness services in Asia. This includes massage therapy franchises, spa concepts, and alternative health services such as acupuncture or chiropractic care.

Mental health and stress management services also present opportunities. As awareness of mental health issues grows in Asia, franchises offering services such as meditation studios or stress management workshops may find increasing demand.

Education and Training

The education and training sector has long been a strong area for franchising in Asia, and this trend is likely to continue with some evolving opportunities.

Early Childhood Education

With increasing emphasis on early childhood development and dual-income families becoming more common in many Asian countries, franchises offering preschool and kindergarten services are likely to see continued growth. Concepts that can offer high-quality, structured early learning experiences with a focus on holistic development are particularly well-positioned.

Supplementary Education

After-school tutoring and enrichment programs remain popular across much of Asia, driven by a cultural emphasis on academic achievement. However, the nature of these programs is evolving. There's growing demand for programs that go beyond traditional academic subjects to include skills like critical thinking, creativity, and emotional intelligence.

STEM (Science, Technology, Engineering, and Mathematics) education franchises are likely to see particular growth. This includes coding academies for children, robotics clubs, and math enrichment programs.

Language Learning

Despite the long-standing presence of English language learning franchises in Asia, this sector continues to offer opportunities. However, the most successful franchises are likely to be those that can offer immersive, technology-enhanced learning experiences rather than traditional classroom-based instruction.

There's also growing demand for other languages, particularly Mandarin Chinese, driven by China's economic influence in the region. Franchises offering Mandarin language instruction to non-Chinese speakers could find significant opportunities.

Professional Training and Upskilling

As the job market becomes increasingly competitive and technology continues to reshape industries, there's growing demand for professional training and upskilling services. Franchises offering courses in areas such as digital marketing, data analysis, or business management are likely to find a receptive market.

Technology and Digital Services

The rapid digital transformation across Asia is creating new opportunities for technology-focused franchises.

Digital Marketing Services

As businesses of all sizes recognize the importance of digital marketing, franchises offering these services to small and medium-sized enterprises (SMEs) are likely to find significant opportunities. This could include franchises specializing in social media management, search engine optimization (SEO), or local digital advertising.

IT Support and Cybersecurity

With the increasing reliance on technology in business operations, franchises offering IT support services to SMEs are likely to see growing demand. This could include on-site support, remote troubleshooting, and managed IT services.

As awareness of cybersecurity threats grows, franchises offering cybersecurity services for small businesses could also find a receptive market.

E-commerce Services

The booming e-commerce sector in Asia is creating opportunities for franchises that can support online sellers. This could include franchises offering services such as product photography, inventory management, or fulfilment services for e-commerce businesses.

Eco-friendly and Sustainable Services

With growing awareness of environmental issues across Asia, franchises offering eco-friendly products and services are likely to see increasing opportunities.

Sustainable Retail

Retail franchises focused on sustainable, eco-friendly products are likely to find a growing market. This could include zero-waste stores, which allow customers to buy products without packaging, or stores specializing in sustainably produced clothing and household goods.

Green Services

Service-based franchises with an eco-friendly focus also present opportunity. This could include eco-friendly cleaning services, using non-toxic cleaning products, or green landscaping services that focus on water conservation and native plants.

Recycling and Upcycling

As awareness of waste management issues grows, franchises offering innovative recycling or upcycling services could find opportunities. This might include franchises that collect and recycle specific types of waste, or those that upcycle waste materials into new products.

Senior Care and Services

With rapidly aging populations in many Asian countries, particularly Japan, South Korea, and China, franchises catering to seniors are likely to see significant growth.

Home Care Services

Franchises offering in-home care services for seniors are likely to see growing demand as many Asian cultures prefer to care for elderly family members at home rather than in institutional settings.

Senior-focused Fitness and Wellness

Fitness and wellness concepts specifically tailored to seniors represent another area of opportunity. This could include low-impact exercise programs, specialized physiotherapy services, or wellness programs focused on maintaining cognitive health.

Senior Social and Lifestyle Services

Franchises offering social activities and lifestyle services for active seniors are also likely to find opportunities. This could include travel services catering to seniors, social clubs, or lifelong learning programs.

Pet Care and Services

The pet care industry is growing rapidly across much of Asia as pet ownership becomes more common and pet owners increasingly treat their animals as family members.

Pet Grooming and Daycare

Franchises offering pet grooming services or daycare facilities for pets are likely to see continued growth, particularly in urban areas where pet owners may not have the time or space to care for their pets during working hours.

Pet Health and Wellness

Veterinary franchises and pet health services represent another area of opportunity. This could include traditional veterinary clinics as well as more specialized services such as pet physiotherapy or alternative health treatments for animals.

Premium Pet Food and Products

With pet owners increasingly willing to spend on high-quality products for their animals, franchises offering premium pet food or eco-friendly pet products are likely to find a receptive market.

The Future of Sector-specific Opportunities in Asian Franchising

As we look to the future, it's clear that the most promising sector-specific opportunities in Asian franchising will be those that align with broader societal trends and changing consumer preferences. Successful franchisors will need to stay attuned to these shifts and be prepared to innovate and adapt their concepts accordingly.

Several overarching trends are likely to shape sector-specific opportunities across the board:

⇒ Technology Integration: Regardless of the specific sector, franchises that can effectively integrate technology to enhance customer experience, improve operational efficiency, or offer new services are likely to have a competitive edge.

⇒ Personalization: Consumers are increasingly expecting personalized products and services. Franchises that can offer customization or tailor their offerings to individual preferences are likely to find success.

⇒ Convenience: In many Asian markets, particularly urban areas, consumers place a high value on convenience. Franchises that can offer time-saving solutions or make their services easily accessible are likely to be well-received.

⇒ Sustainability: Environmental concerns are likely to become increasingly important to Asian consumers. Franchises that can demonstrate a commitment to sustainability in their operations and offerings are likely to resonate with this growing sentiment.

⇒ Health and Wellness: The trend towards healthier lifestyles is likely to continue influencing consumer choices across various sectors, from food and beverage to fitness and personal care.

In conclusion, while traditional sectors like food and beverage and retail will continue to be important in Asian franchising, new opportunities are emerging in sectors aligned with changing consumer preferences and societal needs. Franchisors who can identify these trends early and develop innovative concepts to meet these evolving needs are likely to find significant opportunities in the dynamic and diverse markets of Asia.

Sustainability and Social Responsibility

As environmental concerns and social issues gain increasing prominence across Asia, sustainability and social responsibility are becoming critical factors in the franchising landscape. Consumers, particularly younger generations, are increasingly considering the environmental and social impact of their purchasing decisions. This shift in consumer behaviour is driving franchisors to integrate sustainability and social responsibility into their business models. This section explores the growing importance of these factors in Asian franchising and how they are likely to shape the industry's future.

The Rise of Sustainable Franchising

Sustainable franchising refers to franchise systems that prioritize environmental sustainability in their operations, products, and services. This approach is gaining traction across Asia as consumers become more environmentally conscious and governments implement stricter environmental regulations.

Green Operations

Many franchisors are taking steps to reduce the environmental impact of their operations. This includes implementing energy-efficient practices in stores and restaurants, reducing water usage, and minimizing waste production. For instance, some quick-service restaurant franchises are transitioning to energy-efficient kitchen equipment and LED lighting, while retail franchises are adopting more sustainable packaging and display materials.

In countries like Japan and South Korea, where environmental regulations are particularly stringent, franchisors are often at the forefront of adopting green technologies. This includes the use of solar panels, smart energy management systems, and advanced recycling processes. As other Asian countries continue to strengthen their environmental policies, these practices are likely to become more widespread across the region.

Supply Chains

Franchisors are increasingly focusing on developing sustainable supply chains. This involves sourcing products and materials from suppliers who adhere to environmentally friendly practices, as well as optimizing logistics to reduce carbon emissions.

In the food and beverage sector, for example, many franchises are prioritizing locally sourced, organic ingredients. This not only reduces the carbon footprint associated with transportation but also supports local agricultural communities. Some franchises are going a step further by implementing vertical farming techniques or partnering with urban farms to source ultra-local produce.

Eco-friendly Products and Services

There's a growing market for franchises that specialize in eco-friendly products and services. This includes retail franchises selling sustainable fashion or zero-waste products, as well as service franchises offering eco-friendly alternatives to traditional services.

For instance, eco-friendly cleaning franchises are gaining popularity in urban centres across Asia. These franchises use non-toxic, biodegradable cleaning products and often employ water-saving techniques. Similarly, green beauty salons that use organic, cruelty-free products are finding success in markets like South Korea and Japan, where beauty and skincare are significant industries.

Social Responsibility in Franchising

Beyond environmental sustainability, franchisors are increasingly recognizing the importance of social responsibility. This encompasses a wide range of initiatives aimed at positively impacting local communities and society at large.

Ethical Labour Practices

Ensuring fair and ethical labour practices throughout the franchise system is becoming a key focus for many franchisors. This includes providing fair wages, safe working conditions, and opportunities for career development. In countries like Bangladesh and Vietnam, where labour issues have been a concern in the past, franchisors who can demonstrate strong ethical labour practices are likely to gain a competitive edge.

Some franchisors are going beyond basic compliance to implement progressive labour policies. For example, certain franchises in Japan and Singapore are leading the way in providing flexible working arrangements and comprehensive mental health support for employees. As work-life balance becomes an increasingly important issue across Asia, these practices are likely to become more common.

Community Engagement

Many franchises are implementing programs to engage with and contribute to local communities. This can take various forms, from regular charitable donations to more hands-on community service initiatives.

For instance, some educational franchises in India and Indonesia are offering free classes to underprivileged children as part of their social responsibility initiatives. In the Philippines, certain food and beverage franchises have implemented programs to donate unsold food to local charities, addressing both food waste and hunger issues.

Diversity and Inclusion

Promoting diversity and inclusion within franchise systems is becoming increasingly important. This includes efforts to increase representation of women and minorities in franchise ownership and management roles.

In markets like Malaysia and Singapore, where ethnic diversity is a key feature of society, franchises that can demonstrate a commitment to inclusivity in their hiring and promotion practices are likely to resonate with consumers. Some franchisors are implementing specific programs to support women and minority franchise owners, recognizing that diversity can drive innovation and better connection with diverse customer bases.

The Business Case for Sustainability and Social Responsibility

While the primary drivers for sustainability and social responsibility initiatives are often ethical considerations and consumer demand, there's also a strong business case for these practices in franchising.

Cost Savings

Many sustainability initiatives, particularly those focused on energy efficiency and waste reduction, can lead to significant cost savings over time. For instance, franchises that invest in energy-efficient equipment or implement water-saving measures often see reduced utility costs, which can improve profitability for franchisees.

Brand Reputation and Customer Loyalty

Franchises that demonstrate a genuine commitment to sustainability and social responsibility often enjoy enhanced brand reputation and customer loyalty. This is particularly true in markets like Japan and South Korea, where consumers are increasingly factoring a company's environmental and social practices into their purchasing decisions.

Employee Satisfaction and Retention

Socially responsible practices can lead to higher employee satisfaction and retention rates. This is crucial in markets like Singapore and Hong Kong, where competition for talent is fierce. Franchises that are known for their ethical practices and positive community impact often find it easier to attract and retain high-quality employees.

Challenges and Considerations

While the trend towards sustainability and social responsibility in franchising is clear, it's not without its challenges.

Balancing Costs and Benefits

Implementing sustainable practices often requires upfront investment, which can be challenging for franchisees, particularly in emerging markets. Franchisors need to carefully balance the long-term benefits of these initiatives with the short-term costs to ensure they don't place undue financial burden on franchisees.

Maintaining Consistency

For international franchises operating across multiple Asian markets, maintaining consistency in sustainability and social responsibility practices can be challenging due to varying regulations, cultural norms, and consumer expectations. Franchisors need to develop flexible strategies that can be adapted to local contexts while maintaining the core principles of their sustainability and social responsibility policies.

Avoiding Greenwashing

As consumers become savvier about sustainability claims, franchises need to ensure their initiatives are genuine and impactful. There's a risk of backlash if consumers perceive a franchise's sustainability or social responsibility efforts as superficial or disingenuous.

The Future of Sustainability and Social Responsibility in Asian Franchising

Looking ahead, sustainability and social responsibility are likely to become increasingly central to franchising strategies in Asia. Several trends are likely to shape this evolution:

Regulatory Pressures

As governments across Asia implement stricter environmental regulations and social policies, franchises will need to adapt their practices to ensure compliance. This is likely to drive further innovation in sustainable technologies and practices within franchise systems.

Consumer Expectations

As Asian consumers, particularly younger generations, become more environmentally and socially conscious, their expectations of businesses are likely to rise. Franchises that can authentically demonstrate their commitment to sustainability and social responsibility are likely to gain a competitive edge.

Technological Advancements

Emerging technologies are likely to play a crucial role in enabling more sustainable franchise operations. This could include advancements in renewable energy, waste management technologies, and digital tools for tracking and optimizing resource use.

Circular Economy Models

There's growing interest in circular economy models, which aim to eliminate waste and maximize resource use. Some franchises are already exploring how to incorporate circular economy principles into their operations, such as implementing comprehensive recycling programs or designing products for reuse and recycling.

Social Impact Franchising

We may see the rise of franchises that are specifically designed to address social or environmental issues. These "social impact franchises" could range from businesses focused on providing affordable healthcare or education to franchises specializing in environmental remediation or sustainable agriculture.

In conclusion, sustainability and social responsibility are becoming increasingly important factors in the Asian franchising landscape. As environmental concerns and social issues continue to gain prominence, franchises that can effectively integrate these considerations into their business models are likely to find success. While there are challenges to overcome, the long-term benefits – both for business performance and societal impact – make this a crucial area of focus for franchisors looking to thrive in the evolving Asian market. The franchises that can lead in this area, demonstrating genuine commitment and innovative approaches to sustainability and social responsibility, are likely to be well-positioned for success in the future of Asian franchising.

Cross-border Franchising within Asia

As Asian economies continue to integrate and grow, cross-border franchising within the region is becoming an increasingly significant trend. This section explores the opportunities, challenges, and future prospects of intra-Asian franchise expansion, highlighting the factors driving this trend and the strategies franchisors are employing to navigate the diverse markets within Asia.

Rise of Intra-Asian Franchising

Historically, much of the franchise expansion in Asia has been dominated by Western brands entering Asian markets. However, recent years have seen a marked increase in Asian franchises expanding into neighbouring countries. This trend is driven by several factors, including growing economic integration within the region, rising disposable incomes, and increasing cultural exchange between Asian countries.

Economic initiatives such as the Association of Southeast Asian Nations (ASEAN) Economic Community and the Regional Comprehensive Economic Partnership (RCEP) are fostering greater economic integration within Asia. These agreements are reducing trade barriers and facilitating cross-border business operations, making it easier for franchises to expand across national borders.

For instance, Singapore-based franchises are finding it increasingly straightforward to expand into markets like Malaysia, Indonesia, and Vietnam due to the ASEAN framework. Similarly, South Korean franchises are leveraging trade agreements to facilitate expansion into Japan and Southeast Asian markets.

The rapid growth of the middle class across many Asian countries is creating new opportunities for franchise expansion. As disposable incomes rise, there's increasing demand for the products and services offered by franchises, particularly in sectors like food and beverage, retail, and personal services.

Chinese franchises, for example, are finding success in Southeast Asian markets where there are significant ethnic Chinese populations with growing spending power. Similarly, Japanese lifestyle and retail franchises are resonating with the expanding middle classes in countries like Thailand and Vietnam.

While Asia is incredibly diverse, there are often cultural similarities or affinities between neighbouring countries that franchises can leverage. This cultural proximity can make it easier for franchises to adapt their concepts and marketing strategies when expanding into nearby markets.

For example, Korean franchises in the beauty and fashion sectors have found success expanding into China and Southeast Asia, buoyed by the popularity of Korean pop culture in these regions. Similarly, Taiwanese bubble tea franchises have successfully expanded across much of Asia, benefiting from a shared appreciation for tea-based beverages in many Asian cultures.

Opportunities in Cross-border Asian Franchising

The trend towards intra-Asian franchising presents several key opportunities for franchisors and franchisees alike.

For franchisors, expanding into other Asian markets offers an opportunity to diversify their operations and reduce dependence on their home market. This can be particularly valuable for franchises based in smaller Asian economies, as it allows them to access larger consumer markets and achieve economies of scale.

Cross-border franchising facilitates the transfer of knowledge and best practices between different Asian markets. Franchisors can learn from their experiences in different countries, refining their operations and adapting their concepts to suit diverse consumer preferences.

Expanding into multiple Asian markets can help franchises build stronger, more recognizable brands across the region. This regional brand recognition can be particularly valuable as Asian consumers become increasingly mobile, travelling frequently between countries for business and leisure.

Challenges in Cross-border Asian Franchising

While the opportunities are significant, franchisors expanding within Asia also face several challenges.

Despite efforts towards economic integration, significant regulatory differences remain between Asian countries. Franchisors need to navigate varying legal requirements, tax systems, and business regulations as they expand across borders.

For instance, a franchise expanding from Singapore to Indonesia would need to adapt to very different legal systems, labour regulations, and foreign ownership rules. Similarly, a Chinese franchise entering Japan would need to navigate strict food safety regulations and complex real estate laws.

While there may be cultural affinities between some Asian countries, significant differences in consumer preferences and behaviours still exist. Franchisors need to carefully adapt their products, services, and marketing strategies to suit local tastes and customs.

A prime example is the fast-food sector, where franchises often need to significantly alter their menus to suit local palates. A Filipino fast-food chain expanding into Indonesia, for instance, would need to adapt its offerings to suit Indonesian taste preferences and dietary restrictions.

Expanding across borders often involves dealing with new supply chains, different labour markets, and varying operational norms. Franchisors need to ensure they can maintain quality and consistency across different markets while adapting to local operational realities.

For example, a Japanese retail franchise expanding into Vietnam might face challenges in replicating its highly systematized operational model in a market with different labour practices and supply chain dynamics.

Strategies for Successful Cross-border Asian Franchising

To navigate these challenges and capitalize on the opportunities of intra-Asian expansion, franchisors are employing several key strategies.

Localization

Successful franchisors recognize the importance of adapting their concepts to local markets. This goes beyond simple translation of materials and often involves significant adjustments to products, services, and operational practices.

For instance, some franchisors are creating country-specific menu items or product lines to cater to local tastes. Others are adapting their service models to suit local expectations, such as offering home delivery in markets where this is the norm.

Strategic Partnerships

Many franchisors are forming strategic partnerships with local companies when entering new Asian markets. These partnerships can provide valuable local knowledge, help navigate regulatory hurdles, and facilitate faster market entry.

For example, some Singaporean food and beverage franchises have successfully expanded into China by partnering with local retail groups that provide real estate access and regulatory guidance.

Technology Integration

Franchisors are increasingly leveraging technology to manage cross-border operations more effectively. This includes using cloud-based systems for centralized data management, implementing standardized point-of-sale systems across countries, and utilizing digital training platforms to ensure consistent service standards.

Flexible Franchise Models

Some franchisors are adopting more flexible franchise models to suit different market conditions across Asia. This might involve offering master franchise agreements in some markets while opting for direct franchising in others, depending on local regulations and market characteristics.

Emerging Trends in Cross-border Asian Franchising

Looking to the future, several trends are likely to shape the landscape of intra-Asian franchising.

With the rapid growth of e-commerce and digital services across Asia, we're likely to see more digital-first franchises expanding across borders. These could include e-commerce franchises, online education platforms, or digital service providers that can more easily scale across different markets.

As environmental concerns gain prominence across Asia, franchises with a strong sustainability focus are likely to find opportunities for cross-border expansion. This could include eco-friendly retail concepts, renewable energy service franchises, or sustainable food and beverage brands.

With increasing health consciousness across many Asian countries, franchises in the health and wellness sector are well-positioned for cross-border expansion. This could include fitness concepts, healthy eating franchises, or traditional medicine practices adapted for modern consumers.

As wealth continues to grow in many Asian economies, there's likely to be increased opportunity for luxury and premium franchises to expand across the region. This could include high-end retail concepts, premium dining franchises, or luxury service providers.

The Future of Cross-border Franchising in Asia

As we look ahead, cross-border franchising within Asia is poised to become an increasingly important part of the region's business landscape. Several factors are likely to drive this trend:

Ongoing efforts towards economic integration in Asia, such as the further development of the RCEP and other trade agreements, are likely to facilitate easier cross-border expansion for franchises.

As Asian brands continue to gain strength and recognition, both within the region and globally, we're likely to see more Asian franchises expanding confidently into neighbouring markets.

Continued technological advancements are likely to make cross-border operations more manageable, allowing franchises to maintain consistency and quality across diverse markets more easily.

As Asian consumers become more globally connected, there's likely to be growing appetite for diverse franchise concepts from around the region, creating opportunities for cross-border expansion.

Cross-border franchising within Asia represents a significant opportunity for growth and development in the franchise sector. While challenges remain, particularly in navigating the diverse regulatory and cultural landscapes across the region, franchisors that can successfully adapt their models and leverage local partnerships are likely to find substantial opportunities. As Asian economies continue to grow and integrate, we can expect to see an increasing number of Asian franchise brands becoming regional or even global players, reshaping the franchise landscape both within Asia and beyond.

Conclusion

Key Takeaways

As we conclude our comprehensive exploration of franchising in Asia, it's essential to distil the key insights and lessons learned. This section aims to synthesize the most critical takeaways from our study, providing a concise yet thorough summary of the current state and future prospects of franchising in this dynamic region.

The Unique Nature of Asian Franchising

One of the most crucial takeaways from our study is the recognition that franchising in Asia is distinctly different from franchising in Western markets. The diverse cultural, economic, and regulatory landscapes across Asian countries necessitate a nuanced and adaptable approach to franchise development and management.

In many Asian markets, relationships play a more significant role in business dealings than they typically do in Western contexts. This relational aspect of business often extends to franchise relationships, with franchisors needing to invest more time and effort in building strong, trust-based relationships with their franchisees. This contrasts with the more transactional nature of many Western franchise systems.

Furthermore, the concept of face, or maintaining social standing and reputation, is crucial in many Asian cultures. This cultural norm can significantly impact how conflicts are resolved within franchise systems and how feedback is given and received. Successful franchisors in Asia have learned to navigate these cultural nuances, adapting their communication styles and management practices accordingly.

The Importance of Localization

Another key takeaway is the critical importance of localization in Asian franchising. While maintaining brand consistency is important, franchises that have found success in Asia have typically been those willing and able to adapt their concepts to local tastes, preferences, and cultural norms.

This localization goes beyond mere translation of materials or minor menu adjustments. Successful franchises in Asia often engage in substantial product or service adaptations, sometimes creating entirely new offerings specifically for local markets. For instance, many Western fast-food franchises have found success in Asia by developing menu items that cater to local palates, such as rice-based dishes or locally inspired flavours.

Moreover, localization extends to operational practices as well. Franchisors need to be willing to adapt their standard operating procedures to align with local business practices, labour laws, and consumer expectations. This might involve adjusting service models, modifying store layouts, or adapting marketing strategies to resonate with local consumers.

The Role of Technology in Asian Franchising

Our exploration has highlighted the significant role that technology plays in modern Asian franchising. Asian markets, particularly in East and Southeast Asia, are often at the forefront of technological adoption, and this is reflected in franchise operations.

Many successful franchises in Asia have embraced digital technologies to enhance their operations, improve customer experiences, and streamline management processes. This includes the widespread adoption of mobile ordering and payment systems, the use of data analytics for business intelligence, and the implementation of advanced customer relationship management systems.

Furthermore, technology is playing an increasingly important role in franchise training and support. Many franchisors are leveraging e-learning platforms and virtual reality technologies to provide more effective and efficient training to franchisees and their staff. This trend is likely to continue and accelerate in the coming years, particularly as franchises expand across borders within Asia.

The Growing Importance of Sustainability and Social Responsibility

Our study has also highlighted the increasing importance of sustainability and social responsibility in Asian franchising. As Asian consumers, particularly younger generations, become more environmentally and socially conscious, franchises are under growing pressure to demonstrate their commitment to sustainable practices and social causes.

This trend is manifesting in various ways across different franchise sectors. In the food and beverage industry, for instance, we're seeing a growing emphasis on sourcing sustainable and locally produced ingredients. In the retail sector, many franchises are focusing on reducing packaging waste and implementing more environmentally friendly store designs.

Moreover, franchises are increasingly expected to engage positively with local communities and contribute to social causes. This might involve implementing corporate social responsibility programs, engaging in charitable activities, or providing employment opportunities for disadvantaged groups.

The Potential of Intra-Asian Franchise Expansion

A significant takeaway from our study is the growing potential for intra-Asian franchise expansion. While much of the focus in Asian franchising has historically been on Western brands entering Asian markets, we're now seeing a notable increase in Asian franchises expanding into neighbouring countries.

This trend is driven by several factors, including increasing economic integration within Asia, rising disposable incomes across the region, and growing cultural exchange between Asian countries. As Asian economies continue to develop and integrate, the opportunities for cross-border franchising within the region are likely to grow.

However, it's important to note that expanding within Asia is not without its challenges. Despite geographical proximity and some cultural similarities, Asian countries remain highly diverse in terms of regulations, consumer preferences, and business practices. Franchisors looking to expand within Asia need to approach each market individually, carefully adapting their concepts and strategies to suit local conditions.

The Evolving Regulatory Landscape

Our exploration has underscored the complex and evolving nature of franchise regulations across Asia. While some countries, such as Malaysia and South Korea, have well-developed franchise-specific laws, others rely on general commercial laws to govern franchising activities. Moreover, regulations can vary significantly between countries and are often subject to change as governments seek to balance the promotion of business growth with the protection of local interests.

For franchisors operating in or looking to enter Asian markets, staying abreast of these regulatory developments is crucial. This often requires ongoing legal counsel and a willingness to adapt franchise agreements and operational practices to comply with local laws. The complexity of the regulatory landscape also highlights the value of working with local partners who can provide insight into regulatory nuances and help navigate bureaucratic processes.

The Importance of Cultural Intelligence

Perhaps one of the most overarching takeaways from our study is the critical importance of cultural intelligence in Asian franchising. Success in these markets requires more than just a strong business concept or brand; it demands a deep understanding of local cultures, business practices, and consumer behaviours.

This cultural intelligence needs to permeate all aspects of franchise operations, from initial market entry strategies to ongoing management practices. It involves not only understanding surface-level cultural differences but also grasping deeper cultural values and norms that influence business relationships and consumer behaviour.

Franchisors that have succeeded in Asian markets have typically invested significantly in developing this cultural intelligence. This might involve extensive market research, hiring local talent in key positions, or partnering with local entities that can provide cultural insights. The most successful franchisors view cultural adaptation not as a hurdle to overcome, but as an opportunity to enrich their brand and create truly localized experiences that resonate with Asian consumers.

Franchising in Asia presents both significant opportunities and unique challenges. The region's economic dynamism, growing middle class, and increasing openness to international brands create a fertile ground for franchise growth. However, success in these markets requires a nuanced understanding of local cultures, a willingness to adapt, and a commitment to building strong, trust-based relationships. As Asia continues to evolve and grow, franchising is likely to play an increasingly important role in the region's economic development. For franchisors willing to invest the time and resources to truly understand and adapt to Asian markets, the potential rewards are substantial. The future of franchising in Asia is bright, diverse, and full of opportunity for those prepared to embrace its unique characteristics and challenges.

Final Thoughts on Franchising Success in Asia

As we draw our exploration of Asian franchising to a close, it's fitting to reflect on what truly constitutes success in this dynamic and diverse region. The landscape of franchising in Asia is as varied as the continent itself, presenting a tapestry of opportunities interwoven with unique challenges. This final section aims to distil the essence of what it takes to achieve lasting success in Asian franchising, drawing on the insights and lessons we've uncovered throughout this book.

Embracing Adaptability and Flexibility

One of the most fundamental keys to success in Asian franchising is the ability to adapt and remain flexible. The Asian market is not monolithic; it's a conglomeration of distinct markets, each with its own cultural nuances, consumer preferences, and regulatory environments. Successful franchisors in Asia have demonstrated an exceptional ability to adapt their concepts, operational models, and even their core offerings to suit local markets.

This adaptability goes beyond superficial changes like menu translations or minor aesthetic adjustments. It often involves a fundamental rethinking of the franchise model itself. For instance, a franchise that operates on a standalone store model in its home market might find greater success with a shop-in-shop concept in certain Asian markets where real estate costs are prohibitively high. Similarly, a franchise might need to completely overhaul its supply chain to accommodate local sourcing preferences or regulations.

However, the challenge lies in striking the right balance between adaptation and maintaining brand integrity. The most successful franchises in Asia have managed to adapt significantly to local markets while still retaining the essence of their brand. This delicate balance requires a deep understanding of both the brand's core values and the local market's needs and expectations.

Building Strong Relationships

Another crucial aspect of franchising success in Asia is the ability to build and maintain strong relationships. In many Asian cultures, business is fundamentally relational rather than purely transactional. This means that success often hinges on the strength of the relationships built with franchisees, suppliers, local authorities, and other stakeholders.

For franchisors, this often translates to a more hands-on approach to franchise management. Successful franchisors in Asia typically invest significant time and resources in nurturing relationships with their franchisees. This might involve more frequent in-person visits, more comprehensive training programs, or more collaborative approaches to problem-solving.

Moreover, the importance of relationships extends beyond the franchisor-franchisee dynamic. Successful franchises often cultivate strong relationships with local suppliers, which can be crucial for ensuring consistent quality and managing costs. They also invest in building positive relationships with local communities, recognizing that in many Asian markets, a brand's reputation is closely tied to its perceived commitment to the community.

Investing in Local Talent and Knowledge

A key lesson that emerges from our study is the critical importance of local talent and knowledge. Franchisors that have achieved lasting success in Asian markets have typically made significant investments in recruiting, developing, and retaining local talent.

This local talent brings invaluable insights into market dynamics, consumer behaviour, and cultural nuances that are often difficult for outsiders to fully grasp. Moreover, having local leadership can greatly enhance a franchise's ability to navigate regulatory environments and build relationships with key stakeholders.

Successful franchisors often go beyond just hiring local staff; they empower them to take leadership roles and influence strategic decisions. This might involve creating regional headquarters staffed primarily by local talent or ensuring that local teams have significant input into product development and marketing strategies.

Embracing Technology and Innovation

In many Asian markets, particularly in East and Southeast Asia, consumers are at the forefront of technology adoption. Successful franchises in these markets have recognized this trend and have made technology and innovation central to their strategies.

This technological embrace manifests in various ways. For some franchises, it means developing robust digital ordering and delivery systems to cater to tech-savvy consumers. For others, it involves leveraging data analytics to gain deeper insights into consumer behaviour and preferences. Many successful franchises have also embraced social media and digital marketing strategies, recognizing their outsized importance in many Asian markets.

Moreover, technology is increasingly being used to enhance operational efficiency and maintain quality control across franchise networks. This might involve implementing standardized point-of-sale systems, using AI-powered inventory management tools, or leveraging virtual reality for training programs.

Commitment to Quality and Consistency

While adaptability is crucial, our exploration has also highlighted the importance of maintaining consistent quality across franchise networks. Asian consumers, particularly in more developed markets, often have high expectations when it comes to product quality and service standards.

Successful franchisors have demonstrated an unwavering commitment to maintaining quality, even as they adapt to local markets. This often involves rigorous training programs, regular quality audits, and a willingness to invest in high-quality local suppliers. Many successful franchises have also implemented robust feedback systems, allowing them to quickly identify and address any quality issues that arise.

Long-term Perspective

Another key characteristic of successful franchises in Asia is their adoption of a long-term perspective. Many Asian markets require significant upfront investment and may take longer to yield returns compared to more mature franchise markets. Successful franchisors have demonstrated patience and a willingness to invest for the long term.

This long-term perspective often manifests in a measured approach to expansion. Rather than rushing to open as many units as possible, successful franchisors often focus on ensuring the success of each individual unit. They invest heavily in training and support, recognizing that the success of early units is crucial for building brand reputation and attracting high-quality franchisees.

Moreover, a long-term perspective often involves a commitment to sustainable business practices. As Asian consumers become increasingly environmentally and socially conscious, franchises that have embedded sustainability into their operations are better positioned for long-term success.

Cultural Intelligence and Sensitivity

Perhaps the most overarching factor in franchising success in Asia is the development of deep cultural intelligence and sensitivity. This goes beyond just understanding surface-level cultural differences; it involves developing a nuanced understanding of the values, beliefs, and social norms that shape consumer behaviour and business practices in each market.

Successful franchisors have invested heavily in developing this cultural intelligence. This might involve conducting extensive market research, engaging local cultural consultants, or immersing key personnel in local cultures. They recognize that cultural missteps can be costly, not just in terms of lost sales but in damage to brand reputation.

Moreover, cultural intelligence informs every aspect of franchise operations, from product development and marketing strategies to human resource management and conflict resolution. Franchises that have successfully navigated the complex cultural landscape of Asia have often become deeply embedded in local cultures, viewed not as imports but as integral parts of the local business ecosystem.

In conclusion, success in Asian franchising is multifaceted and complex. It requires a delicate balance of adaptability and consistency, a deep commitment to relationship-building, a willingness to embrace technology and innovation, and an unwavering focus on quality. Above all, it demands a profound respect for and understanding of local cultures and markets.

As Asia continues to evolve and grow, the opportunities for franchising success in the region are boundless. However, these opportunities will increasingly favour those franchisors who approach the market with humility, cultural sensitivity, and a genuine commitment to adding value to local communities. The future of franchising in Asia belongs to those who can seamlessly blend global expertise with local insights, creating franchise systems that are truly greater than the sum of their parts.

The journey of franchising in Asia is ongoing, and the lessons we've explored in this book are not static truths but evolving insights. As the region continues to develop and change, so too will the strategies required for franchise success. For those willing to embrace this dynamic environment, to learn continuously, and to adapt tirelessly, the rewards of franchising success in Asia can be truly extraordinary.

Appendices

Appendix A - Country-specific Franchise Regulations

This appendix provides a comprehensive overview of franchise regulations in key Asian markets. It's important to note that regulations can change, and this information should be verified with local legal experts before making business decisions.

China

Franchise regulation in China is primarily governed by the Regulations on Administration of Commercial Franchises, which came into effect in 2007. Key points include:

- ⇒ Franchisors must have owned and operated at least two outlets for more than one year before franchising.
- ⇒ Franchisors must disclose specific information to potential franchisees at least 30 days before signing a franchise agreement.
- ⇒ Franchise agreements must be in writing and include certain mandatory provisions.
- ⇒ Franchisors must file with the Ministry of Commerce within 15 days of signing their first franchise agreement in China.

The regulatory environment in China can be complex, with various ministries and local governments having overlapping jurisdictions. Foreign franchisors should be particularly aware of regulations regarding foreign investment and intellectual property protection.

Japan

Japan does not have specific franchise laws, but franchising is regulated under various existing laws, including:

⇒ Medium and Small Retail Business Promotion Act
⇒ Antimonopoly Act
⇒ Civil Code

Key regulatory aspects include:

⇒ Franchisors must provide a written disclosure document to potential franchisees at least 7 days before signing a contract or receiving any payment.
⇒ The Japan Fair Trade Commission has issued guidelines on franchise disclosure and fairness in franchise relationships.
⇒ There are no registration requirements for franchisors.

While Japan's regulatory environment is generally considered stable and transparent, foreign franchisors should be aware of cultural norms and business practices that can significantly impact franchise operations.

South Korea

South Korea has comprehensive franchise-specific legislation, primarily the Fair Franchise Transactions Act. Key aspects include:

⇒ Franchisors must register with the Korea Fair Trade Commission before engaging in franchise activities.
⇒ A disclosure document must be provided to potential franchisees at least 14 days before signing a franchise agreement or receiving any payment.
⇒ The franchise agreement must include certain mandatory provisions.
⇒ There are restrictions on unfair trade practices in franchise relationships.

South Korea's franchise regulations are among the most detailed in Asia, with a strong focus on protecting franchisees. Foreign franchisors should be prepared for a high level of regulatory scrutiny.

India

India does not have specific franchise laws, but franchising is governed by various existing laws, including:

⇒ Indian Contract Act
⇒ Consumer Protection Act
⇒ Competition Act
⇒ Foreign Exchange Management Act (for foreign franchisors)

Key regulatory aspects include:

⇒ No mandatory disclosure requirements, but general contract law principles apply.
⇒ Foreign franchisors must comply with foreign direct investment regulations, which vary by sector.
⇒ Intellectual property protection is crucial and should be carefully addressed in franchise agreements.

While India's regulatory environment for franchising is relatively flexible, the complex legal system and variations in state laws can present challenges for franchisors.

Singapore

Singapore does not have specific franchise laws, but franchising is regulated under general commercial laws, including:

⇒ Competition Act
⇒ Consumer Protection (Fair Trading) Act
⇒ Unfair Contract Terms Act

Key points to note:

⇒ No mandatory disclosure requirements or franchisor registration.
⇒ Franchise agreements are governed by general contract law principles.

⇒ Singapore's legal system is based on English common law, providing a familiar framework for many international franchisors.

Singapore's business-friendly environment and robust legal system make it an attractive market for franchisors, but cultural factors should still be carefully considered.

Malaysia

Malaysia has specific franchise legislation, primarily the Franchise Act 1998. Key aspects include:

⇒ Franchisors must register with the Franchise Development Division before offering franchises.
⇒ A disclosure document must be provided to potential franchisees at least 10 days before signing a franchise agreement.
⇒ Franchise agreements must include certain mandatory provisions.
⇒ Annual reports must be filed with the Franchise Development Division.

Malaysia's franchise regulations are relatively comprehensive and aimed at promoting the development of franchising while protecting franchisees.

Indonesia

Indonesia introduced specific franchise regulations in 2007, which have been updated several times. Key aspects include:

⇒ Franchisors must register with the Ministry of Trade before offering franchises.
⇒ A disclosure document must be provided to potential franchisees at least 2 weeks before signing a franchise agreement.

⇒ Franchisors must prioritise the use of domestic goods and services.
⇒ There are limits on the number of company-owned outlets a franchisor can operate.

Indonesia's franchise regulations reflect a desire to balance foreign franchise entry with protection of local businesses. Foreign franchisors should be prepared for requirements to use local content and support local business development.

Thailand

Thailand does not have specific franchise laws, but franchising is regulated under various existing laws, including:

⇒ Civil and Commercial Code
⇒ Trademark Act
⇒ Trade Competition Act
⇒ Foreign Business Act (for foreign franchisors)

Key points to note:

⇒ No mandatory disclosure requirements or franchisor registration.
⇒ Foreign franchisors may need to obtain foreign business licenses depending on their level of involvement in Thailand.
⇒ Intellectual property protection is crucial and should be carefully addressed.

While Thailand's regulatory environment for franchising is relatively flexible, foreign franchisors should be aware of restrictions on foreign ownership in certain business sectors.

Vietnam

Vietnam introduced specific franchise regulations in 2006, which have been updated several times. Key aspects include:

⇒ Franchisors must register with the Ministry of Industry and Trade before offering franchises.

⇒ A disclosure document must be provided to potential franchisees at least 15 days before signing a franchise agreement.

⇒ Franchise agreements must be in writing and include certain mandatory provisions.

⇒ There are restrictions on franchise fees and royalties.

Vietnam's franchise regulations reflect a desire to promote franchising while protecting local businesses. Foreign franchisors should be prepared for requirements related to technology transfer and support for local franchisees.

The regulatory landscape for franchising in Asia is diverse and complex. While some countries have specific franchise laws, others rely on general commercial legislation. Foreign franchisors must carefully navigate these varied regulatory environments, often with the assistance of local legal experts. Moreover, it's crucial to remember that regulations can change, and staying updated on legal developments is essential for long-term success in Asian franchising.

Appendix B - Glossary of Franchising Terms

This glossary provides definitions for common terms used in franchising, with a particular focus on terms relevant to Asian markets. Understanding these terms is crucial for anyone involved in or considering franchising in Asia.

Area Development Agreement: A contract where a franchisee agrees to open a specified number of franchise units within a defined geographic area over a set period.

Area Representative: An individual or entity that represents the franchisor in a specific geographic area, often responsible for selling franchises and providing support to franchisees in that area.

Brand Standards: The set of rules and guidelines that franchisees must follow to maintain consistency across the franchise system.

Conversion Franchise: An existing independent business that converts to a franchised operation.

Disclosure Document: A legal document provided by the franchisor to prospective franchisees, containing detailed information about the franchise opportunity.

Exclusive Territory: A geographic area within which the franchisor agrees not to establish another franchise or company-owned outlet.

Franchise Agreement: The legal contract between the franchisor and franchisee that outlines the terms and conditions of the franchise relationship.

Franchise Fee: An initial, one-time fee paid by the franchisee to the franchisor for the right to operate under the franchise brand.

Franchisee: An individual or entity that purchases the right to operate a business under the franchisor's brand and system.

Franchisor: The company that grants the right to operate a business under its brand and system.

Guanxi: A Chinese term referring to the system of social networks and influential relationships that facilitate business dealings.

Initial Investment: The total amount of capital required to start a franchise, including the franchise fee, equipment, inventory, and working capital.

Intellectual Property: The intangible assets owned by the franchisor, including trademarks, patents, copyrights, and trade secrets.

Keiretsu: A Japanese term referring to a set of companies with interlocking business relationships and shareholdings.

Master Franchise: A franchise arrangement where the master franchisee is given the right to sub-franchise within a specific territory.

Multi-Unit Franchise: An arrangement where a franchisee owns and operates multiple units of the same franchise brand.

Operations Manual: A comprehensive guide provided by the franchisor that details the procedures for running the franchised business.

Royalty Fee: An ongoing fee paid by the franchisee to the franchisor, typically calculated as a percentage of gross sales.

Sub-Franchise: A franchise unit opened by a master franchisee within their designated territory.

Turnkey Operation: A franchise system where the franchisor provides everything needed to start the business, ready for the franchisee to begin operations immediately.

Unit Franchise: A single franchise location operated by a franchisee.

Vendor Approval: The process by which a franchisor approves suppliers for use by franchisees to maintain quality and consistency.

Zoning Laws: Local regulations that determine how property in specific areas can be used for business purposes.

Chaebol: A South Korean term referring to large, family-owned business conglomerates.

Franchise Disclosure Registry: A government-maintained database of registered franchisors and their disclosure documents, common in some Asian countries.

Local Content Requirement: A regulation, common in some Asian countries, requiring franchises to use a certain percentage of locally sourced goods or services.

Trademark License Agreement: A contract granting the franchisee the right to use the franchisor's trademarks in the operation of the franchised business.

Training Program: The initial and ongoing instruction provided by the franchisor to teach franchisees how to operate the business.

Territory: The geographic area in which a franchisee is permitted to operate their franchised business.

Franchise Association: An organization that represents the interests of franchisors and/or franchisees, often providing resources, advocacy, and networking opportunities.

Good Faith: A legal concept requiring parties in a franchise relationship to act honestly and fairly towards each other.

Holdback: A portion of the initial franchise fee retained by the franchisor until the franchisee opens for business.

Non-Compete Clause: A provision in the franchise agreement that restricts the franchisee from operating a similar business for a specified period after the franchise relationship ends.

Renewal: The extension of a franchise agreement for an additional term after the initial term expires.

Site Selection: The process of choosing an appropriate location for a franchised business, often with assistance from the franchisor.

Transfer: The sale or assignment of a franchise from one franchisee to another, typically requiring the franchisor's approval.

Vertical Integration: A business strategy where a company owns or controls its suppliers, distributors, or retail locations, which can impact franchising arrangements.

This glossary provides a foundation for understanding key franchising terms, particularly in the context of Asian markets. However, it's important to note that the precise meaning and application of these terms can vary depending on the specific franchise system, local laws, and cultural context. Always seek professional advice when dealing with legal and business matters related to franchising.